THE TASTE OF

WINE

Jill Goolden

BBC BOOKS

I would like to thank all the supermarkets, wine shops and warehouses for giving me so many opportunities to taste their wines – without their help it would be impossible to write such a book. Also for their valuable help I would like to thank Maureen Ashley, Vicky Bishop, Rose Murray Brown, Christine Campbell, Graham Chidgey, Janet Croall Billington, Richard Goodman, João Henriques, Andrew Henderson, Gary Lipp, Chris Loveday, Hazel Murphy, Tan Harrington and Jeremy Watson.

Published by BBC Books,
a division of BBC Enterprises Limited,
Woodlands, 80 Wood Lane, London W12 0TT

First published 1990

ISBN 0 563 36045 3

Set in Bodoni by Ace Filmsetting Ltd, Frome
Colour sections printed in Great Britain by Lawrence Allen Ltd, Weston-super-Mare
Printed and bound in England by Clays Ltd, St Ives plc, Bungay & Norwich
Colour separations by Technik Ltd, Berkhampsted
Cover printed by Clays Ltd, St Ives plc, Norwich

Contents

Introduction   9

How to find your way around   10
How to taste   11
The main grape varieties   16
A word or two about wine   24
Touching on the slippery slope   26

The best-known wines of the world

Western Europe

France   30

Alsace
Gewürztraminer	32	Pinot Noir	34
Muscat	33	Riesling	34
Pinot Blanc	33	Sylvaner	35
Pinot Gris or Tokay d'Alsace	33		

Bordeaux
Bordeaux Blanc	37	Médoc	40
Bordeaux Rouge	38	Premières Côtes de Bordeaux	40
Entre-Deux-Mers	39	St-Emilion	41
Graves	39	St-Estèphe	41
Margaux	40		

Burgundy
Bourgogne Aligoté	43	Côte d'Or	47
Bourgogne Blanc	44	Hautes-Côtes de Beaune	47
Bourgogne Passe-Tout-Grains	44	Hautes-Côtes de Nuits	48
Bourgogne Rouge	44	Mâcon Rouge	48
Chablis	45	Mâcon-Blanc Villages	48
Côtes de Beaune-Villages	46	Pouilly-Fuissé	49
Côte Chalonnaise	46	St-Véran	49

Beaujolais
Beaujolais Nouveau or Primeur	50	Beaujolais-Villages	51
Beaujolais	50	Cru Beaujolais	51

The Loire

Anjou	52	Pouilly-Fumé	55
Vin de Pays du Jardin		Sancerre	56
de la France	54	Touraine	57
Muscadet	54	Vouvray	57

The Rhône

Vin de Pays des Coteaux			
de l'Ardèche	59	Crozes-Hemitage	60
Vin de Pays des Bouches		Côtes du Lubéron	61
du Rhône	59	Côtes du Rhône	61
Châteauneuf-du-Pape	59	Tavel Rosé	62
Hermitage	60	Coteaux du Tricastin	63

The South-East

		Côtes du Ventoux	63
Coteaux d'Aix-en-Provence	63		
Corbières	64	Vin de Pays de l'Hérault	66
Vin de Corse	65	Coteaux du Languedoc	67
Fitou	65	Minervois	67
Vin de Pays du Gard/Costières		Côtes de Provence	67
de Nîmes	66	Côtes du Roussillon	69

The South-West

Bergerac	69	Vins de Pays des Côtes	
Cahors	70	de Gascogne	72
Côtes du Frontonnais/Fronton	71	Jurançon	73
Gaillac	72	Côtes de St-Mont	74

Italy   75

Barbaresco	76	Merlot	84
Barbera	77	Montepulciano d'Abruzzo	84
Bardolino	77	Orvieto	85
Barolo	78	Pinot Grigio	85
Bianco di Custoza	79	Soave	86
Brunello di Montalcino	79	Teroldego Rotaliano	86
Chardonnay	80	Tocai	87
Chianti	80	Trebbiano	87
Corvo/Sicily	81	Valpolicella	87
Dolcetto	81	Verdicchio	88
Frascati	82	Vermentino de Sardegna	89
Gavi	82	Vernaccia di San Gimignano	89
Lambrusco	83	Vino Nobile di Montepulciano	90
Lugana	84		

Germany   91

Bereich Bernkastel	97	Niersteiner Gutes Domtal	99
Hock Deutscher Tafelwein	97	Piesporter Michelsberg	99
Liebfraumilch	98	Trocken	99
Mosel Deutscher Tafelwein	98		

Spain   103

Cariñena	104	Rioja	109
Costers de Segre/Raimat	104	Rueda	110
La Mancha	105	Terra Alta	111
Navarra	106	Toro	111
Penedès/Torres	107	Valdepeñas	111
Ribera Del Duero	108	Valencia	112

Portugal   114

Arruda	116	João Pires	118
Bairrada	116	Jose Maria da Fonseca	119
Dão	117	Mateus Rosé	120
Douro	118	Vinho Verde	120

Greece   122

Demestica	122	Retsina	123

Austria   124

Grüner Veltliner	125

England   126

English Wine	127

Lebanon   128

Château Musar	128

Eastern Europe 129

Bulgaria

Aligoté	131	Merlot	134
Cabernet Sauvignon	131	Merlot/Gamza Blend	134
Cabernet Sauvignon/Merlot		Misket	134
Blend	132	Muskat	135
Chardonnay	132	Riesling	135
Mavrud	133	Sauvignon	135
Mehana	133		
Melnik	134		

Hungary

Bull's Blood	137

Yugoslavia

Laski Rizling	139

North America 140

Cabernet Sauvignon	142	Sauvignon Blanc/Fumé Blanc	144
Chardonnay	143	White Zinfandel	145
Merlot	144	Zinfandel	146
Pinot Noir	144		

South America 148

Chile

Cabernet Sauvignon	150	Riesling	152
Chardonnay	150	Sauvignon Blanc	152
Gewürztraminer	151		

Argentina

Cabernet Sauvignon	153	Riesling	153
Chenin Blanc	153	Torrontes	154

Australia 155

Cabernet Sauvignon	157	Sauvignon Blanc	160
Cabernet Sauvignon/Shiraz	157	Semillon	160
Chardonnay	158	Semillon/Chardonnay or	
Marsanne	159	Chardonnay/Semillon	
Muscat	159	Blends	161
Rhine Riesling	159	Shiraz	161

New Zealand 166

Cabernet Sauvignon 167   Sauvignon Blanc 168
Chardonnay 167

South Africa 171

Cabernet Sauvignon 172   Roodeberg 173
Chenin Blanc 172

Index 174

Address for Specific Recommendations 176

Introduction

I WOULDN'T CALL myself so much a connoisseur as an enthusiast. I enjoy wine a lot. Certainly through the enjoyment I've learnt a thing or two, or maybe three or four . . . but as far as I'm concerned, the enjoyment's the thing. Every year, hundreds of thousands of people discover the taste of wine for the first time and join the millions of wine fans there are in Britain already. And we all share one thing in common. We like the taste of wine. And through tasting with your head screwed on – that is tasting and thinking about it – it's possible to take the simple enjoyment a stage further.

The fermented juice of the grape makes a drink that in my opinion has no rivals as a partner for food, and very few as a relaxing glass to enjoy with friends. Whatever your taste, know it or not, there are hosts of ideal wines out there for you. Such is the unbelievable range and versatility of the thousand or so different strains of wine-making grapes, that all manner of wonders can be conjured up from the juice: some silky and sweet, some fruity and succulent, some tart and taut, some fat and soft, pungent and concentrated, dry and meaty, delicate and fresh . . . choose your adjectives and I guarantee I'll be able to find a wine to match.

The subtle changes that take place during fermentation, transform one-dimensional grape juice (don't get me wrong, I have nothing against grape juice, it can be delicious at times despite the fact that it's only one dimensional) into an infinitely intriguing drink. Part of the intrigue is, of course, the alcohol, which is a great relaxer and accepted social accessory. The alcohol itself doesn't in fact make a tangible contribution to the taste of wine, but it does to the construction and body; you certainly miss it when it's not there. To date, alcohol-free 'wines' taste empty and hollow, as though their heart has been torn out. There is no doubt that alcohol has its own particular contribution to make to the enjoyment, but only as one of the multitude of essential ingredients.

These ingredients – bouquet, weight, feel, flavour, fruit, acidity, sweetness, tannin, etc., etc. – combine in thousands of different ways to present in each wine a precise and recognisable taste picture. Now, as you may well have noticed if you've read any wine books, the actual *taste* of a wine seldom gets much of a look-in. There are chapters on vineyards and pruning techniques and grape yield and the favourite recipes of the wine-maker's wife, but precious little about the most vital thing of all: what the wine itself is actually like. This could be because, rich though the English language is,

THE TASTE OF WINE

it doesn't have much of a repertoire when it comes to the findings of the taste buds and olfactories. Describing exact tastes and smells, therefore, is not just a challenge to the language, but to the imagination as well.

Nevertheless I decided to take the task on. Having a good grounding in remote control tasting sessions on the *Food and Drink* programme, conjuring up the scents and flavours in a glass from the other side of the television screen, I decided to take the challenge a step further, and draw taste pictures in words of all the wines most widely available in the high street. The object is to give you a pretty clear idea of what a wine is going to be like before you buy it – and to invite you to taste along with me when you get home. If you write to the address given on page 176 you'll receive a list of specific recommendations of wines for you to try.

Tasting is a very personal thing, of course. I have no doubt that the total taste picture of a wine appears rather differently to different people. The subtle shadings will vary and so perhaps will the relative importance of the component parts, but the general outline is the same. It's possible that you will disagree with me about certain details, and that you will have your own descriptions to add to mine. But here they are for you to play with, to use as a basis for your own records if you like. *The Taste of Wine* is intended to entertain, and through that to broaden your experience in and, much more importantly, enjoyment of the world's most delicious drink. The only purpose for making wine is to give pleasure. And the only purpose I have for writing this book is to introduce you to further delights. Even if it leads you on to only one vinous treat you would not otherwise have discovered, I'll feel it was a job well done.

How to Find Your Way Around

THE BOOK is very easy to follow, as it is simply divided into chapters and sections covering the major wine-producing countries of the world, loosely arranged by continent and then country by country. Some countries are subdivided into regions. To find a particular wine, if you know what country and region it comes from, look for it on the contents page where wines are listed alphabetically by the main proper name. (So Vin de Pays des Côtes de Gascogne is listed under G for Gascogne.) If you don't know what country or region it comes from, look for it in the index at the back of the book.

Traditional wine-making countries generally name their wines after places and you will find them within their appropriate chapters listed alphabetically under The Wines and Their Taste. So if you are looking for Minervois, you will find it listed under M within the South-East section of the chapter on France.

Newer wine-producing countries and areas, however, name their wines after the grapes concerned. So do not be surprised to find simply the grape types listed for new world countries. On any new world label, the grape type is the most important information (leaving the brand name aside). To find out about the taste of a new world wine, look for the relevant grape under The Grapes and Their Taste within the appropriate chapter. For example, if you want to find out about a Chardonnay from Australia, look under the main heading of Australia and then C for Chardonnay under The Grapes and Their Taste.

When you find your desired wine, you'll see that the description of the actual taste is in bold type and any background notes are in ordinary type. Only still table wines are included in the book – no sparklers and no dessert wines, I'm afraid – there simply wasn't space. To find a wine to go with a particular meal, look for the food in question in the index to find its ideal partner.

The size of each country's section of the book is determined by the nature of its wine operation and not necessarily by its relative importance on the wine shop shelves. So it is no reflection, for example, on Australia's wines and what we think of them that her chapter is comparatively short; this is because her wines are so easy to classify and pigeon hole. France, on the other hand, is much longer and more complicated because every wine from every region has a different name and a different pedigree, owing to the fact that, when her wine industry was established, there was no communication between different regions. Each, therefore became an independent microcosm, using idiosyncratic grape varieties and making them into thoroughly different tasting wines sold under completely different names.

How to Taste

 BEING AT IT, as it were, all the time, I never give a second thought to the mechanics of wine tasting. A parallel is driving a car; once you've mastered the gears, you never bother to think about them again – there's much too much to get on with just making your way around the roads. And so it is with tasting wine. The peering, swirling, sniffing, slurping, gargling, spitting business is the equivalent of gear changing; the means to the end, and that end, of course, is simply enjoying wine to the full.

The routine of examining a glass of wine in great detail is, it must be said, an unglamorous one, and certainly not one to be entered into except among like-minded adults. But knowing how to get the wine to tell you absolutely everything there is to say about itself is a good trick, and a necessary one if you're going to take your wine appreciation and recognition a step further than simply enjoying the odd glass.

The purpose of all the various contortions is to use to the full the tasting gear with which we are all equipped. If you just raise a glass to your lips, take a swig and swallow, the wine races down your throat without even having made the acquaintance of half your essential taste sensors. Bad design (of the mouth, that is) you may say, but I think not. It works quite adequately if unhurried, and quite magically if you co-operate as best you can to make sure every bud, every nerve has the chance to register its impressions and communicate them to the taste memory bank in your brain.

Let me talk for a moment about the anatomy of the nose and mouth and how each bit is intended to work. The nose is there to smell, of course, and has a direct route for communicating its findings to a special part of the brain. When you sniff at a glass of wine, the volatile elements whistle up your nostrils where they come into contact with the olfactory nerves in the lining of the upper part of the nostril. These nerves communicate instantly with the memory bank in the brain and identify (if you are lucky, or have an extremely well-stocked memory bank) that particular smell.

The nose is a pretty reliable appendage and good at recalling previous encounters with a particular scent. You know how evocative certain smells can be, how they instantly transport you to an event in your past. For animals living in the wild, a strong sense of smell, coupled with immediate interpretation of any given whiff, is vital to survival – much more important than a sense of taste – and to an extent we have held on to that instinctive ability. It must be used, though, or it dims and the memory bank becomes somewhat impoverished.

The recognition of a certain aroma, therefore, is immediate. One deep sniff will tell you as much as you are ever going to know. In fact, after the first impression, the scent seems to fade and the nose's perceptiveness runs out of puff. So the technique is to breathe in the bouquet deeply, do your best to interpret what you find and move on to the taste. But the role of the nose is not over yet . . .

The mouth, as you know, contains taste buds for deciphering tastes. These are mainly located on the tongue, with some scattered on the soft palate at the back of the roof of the mouth. A quick gulp of a liquid does not give the buds a chance to analyse the sundry flavours, which they must if you are going to get a complete picture of the whole taste. So if you are really trying to taste a wine thoroughly, you must take a good mouthful and swill it round to make sure all the taste buds are involved. Even then, though, they do a fairly feeble job on their own. To do their absolute best they need to work in conjunction with your nose and your more perceptive sense of smell.

When you have a heavy cold, you know how badly your sense of taste is affected. That's because it's struggling to work on its own without involving your sense of smell. If you've watched a wine taster, or even a tea, coffee or lemonade taster, at work, you may have been appalled at the mannerless sound effects as they slurp their way (okay I'll admit it, slurp our way) through each mouthful. The reason is that we are trying to get as many vapours into the nasal passages as possible while containing the liquid in the mouth, so as to have a two-pronged attack from taste buds and olfactory nerves simultaneously. This gives you the best chance possible of analysing and appreciating the taste.

But before you conjure up visions of me gargling at the dinner table, doing my 'demented ostrich' bit bobbing my nose in and out of the glass next time I'm in the pub, let me say that all the ritual associated with examining wine in such detail is necessary only when actively *tasting* wine as opposed to just drinking it. I enjoy having a glass with friends socially, too, when I can assure you there is no peering, swirling, sniffing, gargling and slurping at all. Not one bit. That is reserved for scrutinising a wine in private or with other 'tasters' to judge its quality, see how well made it is, if it's worth the money or, on the occasions when I am subjected to blind 'guess the identity' tastings, to try to discover what on earth it is . . . and then I can assure you, I need all the help I can get.

If you do decide to have a go at the tasting ritual, let me warn you that to begin with you feel a bit of a nut case going through all the necessary contortions, but you'll find that they *do* work; here's how.

A glass with a stem and a bowl that curves in at the top is a necessary piece of equipment. The ordinary Paris goblet is fine (the shape you find most often in pubs and cheap-and-cheerful restaurants) or you can use the tulip design. The reason these are the best shapes for a tasting glass is described in steps 1, 2 and 3. So here goes:

Step 1

Fill the glass about a third full (no more); never higher than the widest part of the Paris goblet. It's best to handle the glass by the stem so as not to alter the temperature of the wine inside and to keep your sticky finger prints off the bowl of the glass; you can see it better then. If you are going to taste many wines on one occasion, you can use the same glass for each wine as long as you don't warm it up or dirty the sides.

Step 2

Look at the colour of the wine. You can best do this either by holding the glass up and looking at the contents against a white background, or to see in more detail, you tilt the glass and look down at the wine lying in the curve of the bowl against a white tablecloth or piece of white paper. Red wines change from being purply red when young to becoming a little rusty, with a darker rim when more mature. White wines vary from being almost as white as water to old gold in an older wine, or one that has been aged in wood – so the colour helps you judge the age and possibly the style of the wine. The general rule for both red and white wines is the paler the wine the lighter bodied it will be and the darker, the fuller bodied.

Step 3

Holding the glass by the stem, swirl the wine round in the bowl, disrupting the surface. This is quite an art, and can be fairly hazardous when you first try. To play safe, you can keep the base of the glass on the table while you swirl, or just content yourself with jiggling the glass enough to break the wine's surface. This releases the aromas into the bowl of the glass where they are trapped because of the narrowing of the glass towards the opening. The reason for filling the glass only a third full is to leave plenty of room for the wine to ripple and for the released aromas to collect – and of course to leave room for you to insert your nose. Immediately after your brief swirl, you must get your nose right down into the glass and draw your breath in deeply, giving a good sniff. Because your sense of smell is so short-lived, give a long pause before going back to nose the wine again.

Step 4

Now for the first taste. It is alleged by some that different areas of the tongue pick up different types of taste. There are only five essential tastes, of which three are relevant to wine tasting: sweetness, which is supposedly picked up on the tip of the tongue; acidity, which is picked up on the upper edges; and bitterness which is sensed at the back. So to register all these tastes, you must make sure all parts of your tongue come into contact with the wine. Less well known is the fact that your sense of smell can be used as a 'booster' while you taste the wine. The trick here is to breathe in air through the mouth *while* tasting the wine and coating all your taste buds . . . here's how. Take a good-sized sip and 'chew' the liquid round in your mouth. Don't swallow! While the mouthful of wine is still being held on top of your tongue, open your lips as though about to whistle, and suck in little gusts of air, which should pass over the wine, carrying the vapours to the back of your throat where your sense of smell can pick them up. (You have to be careful experimenting with this technique at first, since if you catch the wine with the air, you can choke.)

Step 5

If you were to be going on to taste lots of wines after this mouthful and wanted to keep your wits about you, this would be the time to spit the wine out, if not, then swallow. It is actually entirely possible – especially after a bit of practice – to taste a wine thoroughly and completely without actually swallowing it. This may seem to destroy all the fun, but is a necessary sacrifice to make if you are planning to study a number of wines. The key thing when spitting out a mouthful of wine is to be positive. You have to spit forcefully, and curiously the more force you put behind it, the tidier and more accurate you are. A good place to practise is the bathroom. With water, not wine.

So there you have the technique. Recording what you actually discover during all these contortions is a different matter altogether. Professional wine tasters jot down their tasting notes on paper, many of them, I sneakingly suspect, using some highfaluting wine speak. But you don't have to embark on a whole new language course to record your thoughts about wines. Your normal vocabulary will do just as well. There are wildly conflicting opinions about how wines should be described. There are those who disdain what they call the 'bubblegum school' of wine description – that is the likening of wines to everyday scents and flavours such as bubblegum (well not everyday in my case, but you know what I mean).

Often wines seem to echo the scents and flavours associated with fruits and flowers

– and why not? The grapes from which wine is made are fruits, after all, and whether or not they smell and taste immediately fruity (and let's be realistic, lamentably often they don't), it is a fact that all wines share with fruit and vegetables common traces of acids, alcohols and other components. They're all in the same family, after all.

The purpose of allocating easily recognisable, everyday memory triggers to wines is twofold. First they are scents and flavours universally recognised, and second, if a certain smell or taste in a wine recalls bubblegum, go for it, log it in the memory bank. It means that the next time you come across that smell or taste, you'll instantly recognise it. I'm not for a moment meaning to imply that the wine is flavoured by or even like bubblegum. But if that is one of the flavours recalled by the taste of the wine, then remarking on it helps to build up a complete and memorable taste picture of what you have in the glass.

You only have to read a couple of lines of the tasting notes in this book to realise that I am a committed-up-to-the-eyebrows pupil of the bubblegum school. I always feel cheated when I find that the taste of a wine is simply not described in a book devoted to the subject (and it virtually never is). What good is, and I quote, 'elegant and close knit, perky and slightly assertive. Charming and definitely well bred'? It could be a thumb-nail sketch of the royal family . . . a fat lot it tells you about the taste of a particular wine (it was a Champagne, as it happens).

As far as I am concerned the taste is the crux of the whole matter. And for my purposes, I try to describe it as best I can so that anyone reading the notes can imagine what the wine is like. For your own purposes, you only have to 'know what you mean' (and know what you like). Essentially the things you are looking for are bouquet and taste.

Bouquet

Does this wine have a powerful aroma, a delicate aroma, virtually no smell at all? Is the 'bouquet' pleasant? Fruity? Flowery? Earthy? Vegetably? Smoky? Chemical? Does it remind you of another scent? The red Cabernet Sauvignon grape, for instance, can smell powerfully of blackcurrants, and the Sauvignon Blanc of gooseberries, and these are triggers you soon log.

Taste

Here, again, you are looking for identifiable characteristics. When you first taste the wine, does it seem 'fruity' (it is, after all, made from fruit, but does this show?). Is the taste clean from start to finish, or are there some other 'off flavours' creeping in? Has it got a fresh nip of acidity, too much (which makes it rather sharp), or too little (which makes it rather 'soupy' and bland)? In a red wine, can you taste the tannin? Tannin is present in the skin and stalks of the grapes, and imparts body and helps preserve red wines intended to mature for a few years. Ideally, a wine with a lot of tannin (which gives a drying sensation on the sides of your tongue and tastes a bit bitter) should have matured sufficiently for the tannins to have mellowed and married with the other flavours. Tannin shouldn't dominate the fruit. Are all the flavours in harmony with each other, giving a balanced whole? Or do they stand up to be noticed on their own? Can you feel the acidity? (You shouldn't be able to.) What scents and flavours are you reminded of? Are they nice? Do they work? And above all, *do you like it? Is it worth the money? Will you buy it again?*

The Main Grape Varieties

 THE SIMPLE DEFINITION of wine is 'the fermented juice of grapes', not rhubarb or carrots or rice; when fermented, these too will make an alcoholic drink, but it will not in the strict sense of the word be 'wine'. Wine comes only from grapes, and a particular sort of grape at that. There are different vine species native to all parts of the world, of which only one is ideal for wine-making, *vitis vinifera*, generally considered to be Europe's native species. Pulverising the grapes from your fruit bowl and fermenting their juice would not do. Dessert grapes are not in the same family as those of the hallowed (well hallowed by wine-makers anyway) *vitis vinifera* genus used for making wine. They taste much too appealing, for a start.

To make good wine, you do not simply need nectar-sweet juice; that alone would make appalling wine, more like sweet soup. Sweetness is a necessary part of the wine-making grape, but in order to make good wine it must be balanced by acidity and possibly supported by the preserving element of tannin. Wine-making grapes are generally quite small, thick skinned and rather tough and bitter tasting. Virtually all of them have white (well actually green) pulp and juice; the colour in black or red grapes is only in the skins.

Vitis vinifera is believed to have originated in the Middle East, but was gradually adopted by Europe, where it adapted to the varied growing conditions and requirements of different areas. The hundreds of classic 'European' grape varieties that evolved are now being grown and used for wine-making all over the world. (Ironically, to combat the widespread vine devastation wrought by the small louse the phylloxera at the end of the last century, most *vitis vinifera* vines in Europe and in various other parts of the world have been grafted on to phylloxera-resistant American rootstock. They are therefore thoroughly cosmopolitan, but that is by the by.)

Although there are a thousand or so different grape varieties responsible for making wine, you'll be relieved to hear that you do not have to remember them all to be able to recognise the various scents and flavours encapsulated in the bottles on the wine shelves. Far from it; only about fifty varieties of grapes are considered to impart a unique, identifiable taste to the wine, and you can count the essential players on the fingers of two hands. Less vital varieties (to remember, that is) could take you on to your toes, too, but you'll certainly have run out of the varieties with more than minor significance before you've made it to twenty.

The grape world is a diminishing one. As wine buyers become more familiar with the classic varieties whose names appear on wines from the 'new world' of wine (Americas, Australia and New Zealand) as well as increasingly on wines from fashionable 'new' (well new to us anyway) areas of the old world, so these varieties spread, with wine-makers in traditional areas wanting a slice of the fashionable limelight. A handful of popular varieties are now being planted all over the world, and in many instances ousting the obscure local grape varieties that were once planted there.

So here are little thumb-nail sketches of the principal grape varieties. Some (although I haven't identified them as such, I don't want to hurt any feelings) I consider second division varieties, those accustomed to making traditional wines in precise areas – and delicious and good value many of them are, too – but they are not buzz names on the wine shelves; indeed you'll virtually never see their names on the label. Wines made in the old, traditional areas are generally named after a place, not the grape, and these local grape types have not been sought out for introduction to the 'new world' of wine. I think you'll spot them when you come to them.

Not all grape varieties make wines on their own; many famous wines are blends of two, three, or even of several different varieties. Most Champagnes, for instance, are blends of three different types of grapes: two black – one major and one minor – and one white. In general, blending is more usual in the making of red wines than with whites, although there are some famous marriages between white grapes, such as Sémillon and Sauvignon.

White Grapes:

Chardonnay

Chardonnay is certainly the most fashionable white grape variety today. Historically, white Burgundies have been regarded as the best white wines in the world, and the Chardonnay grape is behind all the classics (although it doesn't say so on the label). It is also the only white variety used to make Champagne – performing on its own in all *blanc de blancs* (literally 'white of whites', meaning white wine of white grapes; other Champagnes include the juice of black grapes, too). Chardonnay is now nurtured to a lesser or greater extent in virtually every other wine-producing region, and labels of these 'new' wines proclaim its presence loud and clear. It is a particular favourite in Australia, where an intense, rich (though not sweet) style of Chardonnay is general – often aged in wood to give 'patisserie' notes, and likewise to a lesser extent on America's West Coast. In northern Italy, it makes light, refreshing wines; in Bulgaria, some disappointing examples, some true, some over-oaked; examples from southern

France are highly variable; those from north-eastern Spain are generally rich and good; from New Zealand, delicate and complex; South American ones occasionally coarse. It is also grown in South Africa. Chardonnays the world over are generally easy to appreciate, where they fall into the subtle, delicate 'appley' class or the mouth-filling, rich, buttery camp at the other end of the scale. And there is no end to the surprises different Chardonnays can spring.

Riesling

Until a very recent law was passed, Rieslings have suffered from confused identity. All manner of so-called 'Rieslings' (Welsch-, Laski-, Olasz-, Italico- with Gray- and Emerald- in California) are bandied about on labels of bottles that contain not a drop of Riesling – that is *real* Riesling – wine inside them. These other Rieslings bear no relationship to the classic master grape of the Rhine and Mosel and henceforth must be called Rizlings to make the distinction. Real Riesling, also known outside Europe as Rhine or Johannisberg Riesling, challenges Chardonnay as the top white wine producing grape, notably in Germany. And precisely because of its success there, it is banned from being planted in France more than thirty miles from the German border. Happily, this region contains the French wine region of Alsace, where the Riesling produces delicate, dry, floral-scented wines with an unmistakable 'petrolly' edge to them. In Germany, Riesling is responsible for the country's best wines, ranging from dry to the unbelievably sweet Trockenbeerenauslesen and also accounting for the best 'mediums' in between. It is popular in America and Australia, where it again produces all styles of wine from the dry side of medium to the richly sweet, and is also grown in South America, South Africa and Eastern Europe. Everywhere it goes it takes with it that floral bouquet, flowery flavour and a fresh zip of acidity.

Sauvignon Blanc

If you stick your nose in a glass of wine and get a whiff of gooseberries, or even of cats (there *is* a family resemblance), it's Sauvignon Blanc. On its own, the Sauvignon makes often rapier sharp wines, always drunk young when you can feel the appley acidity. It is the grape behind those fashionable Loire wines, Sancerre and Pouilly-Fumé (although the label doesn't say so), and Sauvignon de Touraine and Sauvignon-de-St-Bris from Burgundy. It has travelled successfully to the 'new world' – America, South America, Australia and New Zealand – where it often produces richer wines with more body (usually contributed by the added dimension of oak). And outside France it is virtually always dry. But not so in Bordeaux, where it combines magically with the Sémillon grape to produce the greatest sweet wines in the world. Most of the Bordeaux sweeties (including Sauternes and Barsac, of course) are products of this marriage, as are Monbazillacs. Most dry white Bordeaux (such as Entre-Deux-Mers) are also parented by this partnership, with Sémillon dominating, although some (and they may say so on the label) are made from the Sauvignon alone.

Sémillon

The Sémillon is a very surprising grape. Poorly vinified, it makes a blousy, flabby white wine lacking the essential cutting edge. Sometimes it is perked up by blending with another variety, usually in its principal home of Bordeaux, with the Sauvignon. This marriage can then carry the wine to illustrious heights, being responsible for the tremendous sweet white treats of Sauternes and Barsac (as well as from the good value dessert wines from nearby Monbazillac in Bergerac). It also parents most dry Bordeaux. Traditionally Sémillon would dominate the Sémillon/Sauvignon blend, but the thirst for 'crisp dry white wines' has increased the Sauvignon's share considerably. In Bordeaux, of course, in common with most of classical France, the grape never declares itself on the label. But that is by no means the end of the Sémillon story. This ancient grape variety is now widely planted throughout the world, producing anything from slight, even 'green' wines in the cooler climates of New Zealand and the northern states of West Coast America to chunky wood-aged thunderbolts in Australia where the Sémillon is frequently blended with the Chardonnay. The best of the Sémillons (declaring themselves loud and clear on the label) from Australia, notably the Hunter Valley, are rich, rounded, voluptuous wines in the genre of southern hemisphere Chardonnays . . . only more so.

Chenin Blanc

Yet another thoroughly well-travelled variety, the Chenin Blanc performs differently everywhere it goes. Even in its native Loire, it is the grape behind a wide range of wine styles. A large catchment of ordinary Loire dry white wines such as white Anjou, Vouvray and Saumur are produced by the Chenin – regrettably often Chenin heavily overlaid with sulphur. The classic sweeter style Vouvrays come from this grape, too, which easily handles the full range on the dryness-sweetness scale, encompassing the richly honeyed dessert wines of Coteaux du Layon and Moulin Touchais, too. Sparkling Vouvrays, both dry and sweeter, and sparkling Saumurs are made from this grape. All these wines share a common tasting note which is not very attractive to describe but is easy to recognise (and not nearly as off-putting as it sounds); they have a faint 'sicky' scent on the bouquet. The Chenin makes flowery wines, apparently honeyed even when they are dry. In California, the grape has been extensively used to make inexpensive white plonk, but its versatility is now recognised and some dry and sweet treats are beginning to emerge (with the grape on the label, unlike in France). New Zealand has put a lot of vineyard under Chenin Blanc, which likes the cooler climate, and South Africa has made much of its Steen wines (their name for Chenin Blanc).

Müller-Thurgau

Müller-Thurgau hardly ever appears on any but English wine labels, although it is the most planted grape variety in Germany. It was developed by a Dr Müller by crossing the Riesling and Silvaner grape types and it was intended to be as easy to grow as the aristocratic Riesling. That it is, but it certainly doesn't have the ability to make such fine wines. They tend, instead, to be rather insipid, sugary and lacking grip or guts – although good wine-makers can work miracles (as they can with most grape types if they really try). The Müller-Thurgau is behind the majority of 'medium white' wines from Germany and has also travelled fairly extensively abroad, notably to New Zealand, Austria, northern Italy and Eastern Europe.

Muscat

Surprisingly few wines actually smell of grapes – with the rare exceptions of the multifarious products of the Muscat variety. Unlike virtually every other variety of *vitis vinifera*, you could well have come across Muscats in a fruit bowl or dried as muscatels, and they are rich, sweet, pungent grapes which retain their essential characteristics when made into wine. There are actually all manner of Muscat grapes made into wine throughout the world, ranging from small and white to rotund and black, all giving the same musky, sweetly scented, fruity wines. Usually the grape variety is associated with the name on the label, as in the dry Muscats of Alsace and the Lisbon area of Portugal (João Pires dry Muscat). When made into a dry wine, the aromatic medley is retained, suggesting rich juicy ripe fruit, but the taste, although richly scented, is dry. It is in its sweet incarnations that Muscat is most famous, however, as Italy's sparkling Asti and Moscato Spumantes, as France's famous *vins doux naturels* such as Muscat de Beaumes de Venise and Muscat de Frontignan and as Australia's 'late picked Muscats'. There are sweet Muscats from Greece, where the earliest recordings of the grape are found, and from Valencia in Spain. Its incarnations are endless – luckily you can spot them from the label.

Trebbiano/Ugni Blanc

One of the most prolific grape varieties in the world, the Trebbiano, or Ugni Blanc grape as it is known in France, accounts for the lion's share of white wines in two of the world's greatest wine-producing nations, Italy and France. Volume is the thing here. It is a grape variety that can be relied upon to produce quantities of grapes come what may. So although it is responsible for producing some rather characterless wines, at least they have that welcome zing of acidity. In Italy, you'll hardly be able to think of a popular white wine that does not include the ubiquitous Trebbiano; it's in Soave, Orvieto, Frascati, Verdicchio and Galestro from Tuscany, where it even creeps into red Chianti. In France, the grape's principal and traditional use has been to make wine for distillation into brandy – notably Cognac and more recently Armagnac. It is an indictment of the grape that the general rule for distillation is the less pleasant the base wine, the better will be the brandy. Not all Ugni Blanc wines are actively unpleasant, of course; the error of most is that they make little impression at all, whether it be pleasant or unpleasant. It does well, however, in Vin de Pays des Côtes de Gascogne, and spreads across the south of France to Languedoc-Roussillon and Provence. Although never declared on the front label of any bottle anywhere that I know, it is also widely planted in the Americas, Australia and South Africa.

Red Grapes:

You need to remember that red wines are often blends of several different varieties, so expect quite a bit of cross referencing in this section.

Cabernet Sauvignon

The most famous, best travelled red grape variety, Cabernet Sauvignon is now probably grown in every wine-producing country in the world. It has a distinctive juicy blackcurrant scent and flavour, which may be balanced on the palate by tough tannins. Traditionally, wines using this grape variety were made to keep, the maturing process taking many years, during which time the tannin content would soften and marry in. 'New world' Cabernet Sauvignons, generally made in hotter climates than Bordeaux, tend to be made to mature sooner, accentuating the fruity character of the grape and restraining the tannins. Some humbler wines made from this variety can be disappointing and uncharacteristic. The 'ancestral seat' of the Cabernet Sauvignon is Bordeaux, and more precisely the Graves and the Médoc where, blended with some Merlot and Cabernet Franc, it is responsible for making some of the most famous wines in the world, known in Britain as clarets. It stretches out into nearby Bergerac, where it is usually blended in the same way but makes a somewhat coarser marriage. In the Loire it may work with Cabernet Franc to produce both reds and rosés, being the team behind Cabernets d'Anjou. It has been introduced fairly recently into the south of France, where it may boost a traditional blend, or perform on its own and be boasted on the label. It is a famous member of Bulgarian wine circles, and is a new asset for Portugal and Spain, too. Italian so-called Cabernets usually include both Cabernet Sauvignon and Cabernet Franc. And anyone who has ever perused a wine shelf anywhere will realise that it is a mainstay of the wine industries of Australia (where it is also often blended with Shiraz), New Zealand and North and South America. It has even found its way successfully into the Lebanon, where it is incarnated in Château Musar.

Cabernet Franc

The Cabernet Franc is understandably linked closely to Cabernet Sauvignon – in fact on the vine it looks quite similar – and is frequently blended with it. It has a distinctly grassy bouquet, earthy, too. There is good fruit on the palate – more like raspberries, this time. When acting on its own, it is often vinified to make light, lively, youthful wines (as in many Loire reds) which can be served chilled. It has neither found as much fame as the Cabernet Sauvignon and nor has it, as a consequence, travelled as extensively. It's no country bumpkin, though, as it is much used in the making of claret in Bordeaux, particularly in the areas of St-Emilion and Pomerol. It is also found in nearby Bergerac. In the Loire it is the main red variety, anonymously making most of the red wines and joining the Cabernet Sauvignon to make the rosé Cabernet d'Anjou. In Italy it is present in most red Cabernets and is also used in Chile and Eastern Europe to contribute to their claret taste-alikes.

Merlot

Another star in the Bordeaux galaxy that has not made much headway around the world, Merlot produces lovely velvety soft wines with a slight sweet tinge. On the bouquet there can be a piercing floral, almost minty note. Its strength is frequently considered its ability to bring softness to blends including harder, more tannic varieties such as Cabernet Sauvignon. In Bordeaux, it shines brightest in Pomerol and St-Emilion, where it dominates. It has travelled to imaginative vineyards in southern France, which frequently boast of its presence on the label. In Italy it is responsible for some inexpensive, soft reds from Veneto and more serious versions from Friuli; it has been adopted by Bulgaria and Romania and has also crept, in a small way, into California.

Pinot Noir

The Pinot Noir is a very choosy grape variety which adapts poorly to being made to perform outside its native Burgundy, where it is the only grape allowed for fine red wines. There it produces stylish medium bodied wines that have a sweet strawberry fruitiness when young. As they age, they take on some vegetal notes (even composty, sometimes) and become pungently gamey as they mature still further. The best examples are rich and succulent with very subdued tannins and long lasting flavours. It is also – perhaps unexpectedly – the backbone grape of Champagne, which is generally made from two black grapes and one white. The only other place in France you're likely to find it is in Alsace where all red wines are made from the Pinot Noir. It makes some red wines in Germany under the assumed name of Spätburgunder, and in Italy, where it calls itself Pinot Nero. England, bless her heart, has adopted the tricky Pinot Noir for most of her reds (surprisingly good sometimes, in a very light style). Romania makes a good job of it, too, while California, Oregon and Washington State are all persevering to make the definitive non-Burgundian Pinot, and Australia and New Zealand are just beginning the quest.

Gamay

Think of the juicy-fruit scents and flavours of Beaujolais and you have the Gamay. There is a whiff of rubber to the bouquet – like gym shoes running on a hot road – and a suggestion of cherries, cut by an assertive acidity. Gamay wines are light and straightforward. In most, the fruitiness is concentrated by the *macération carbonique* method (see page 26). Acidity is high, giving the wines an apparent liveliness in the mouth. Pale purple in colour, apart from some of the more expensive *Cru* Beaujolais, they are at their best in the first year after they are made; most Beaujolais Nouveau is consumed within weeks. Very similar in style to Beaujolais, red Mâcon is also Gamay based; and also from Burgundy, Passe-Tout-Grains includes a proportion, too. Gamays also come from the Loire, notably Gamay de Touraine and Anjou Gamay, while southern France has her (small) share, especially in the Ardèche.

Syrah

Known as the Shiraz or the Hermitage in Australia, the Syrah grape is responsible for making some big, dark, earthy, 'hot country' reds with complex fruit (often incorporating a fruitgum tang) and a peppery edge. The aroma of creosote has been linked with this grape; wines made from it share that penetrating tarry get-up-your-nose character. In Australia, the Shiraz, so called, makes rich but beefy wines with almost a sweetness to them on the finish. They are renowned for their forthcoming bouquet, likened in Oz to a 'sweaty saddle'. The Shiraz is also often seen in combination with the Cabernet Sauvignon, fleshing it out and beefing it up. But the real home of the Syrah is the northern Rhône, where it is responsible for Hermitage, Crozes-Hermitage, Côte Rôtie, Cornas and St-Joseph. Included in the vinous cocktail that goes to make Côtes du Rhônes (coming largely from the south of the Rhône area), it is also one of the thirteen grape varieties in Châteauneuf-du-Pape. In the traditional 'quantity-rather-than-quality' areas of Midi and Provence, it is sometimes used to lift the tone of blends of the other southern French grapes of Grenache, Carignan and Cinsault. And it also crops up, surprisingly, in the Lebanon, where it is a component of the remarkable Château Musar.

Grenache

Grenache is responsible for making easy drinking, quick maturing, short-lived wines in the south of France to which it gives fruit, a recognisably dusty taste and a sprinkling of pepper. The variety originated in Spain, where it is called Garnacha (a component of Rioja and, incidentally, Spain's most popular red grape variety). On its own, it produces alcoholic wines with little finesse, so it is frequently blended. It is one of the many permitted varieties in Côtes du Rhône and Châteauneuf-du-Pape, dominating the rosés of Tavel and Lirac and the reds and rosés of Provence. You won't see it on the label in Britain, but Australia and California also grow a lot for use in cheap blends.

Nebbiolo

Also known as Spanna, the Nebbiolo grape makes inky dark, thunderously big, tough heavy wines which give a dry feeling to the inside of the mouth (due in part to the high tannin levels and in part to the 'dry' nature of the fruit). These are characterised by northern Italy's Barolos, Barbarescos and Gattinaras; wines worth waiting for, they take a few years to 'come round' after they are made. The Nebbiolo isn't intended for immediate drinking.

Tempranillo

It is difficult to describe the Tempranillo without considering oak. Wood-aged Tempranillo (and most of it is) has the rich, sweet scent and flavour of fruit and vanilla or fruit and custard, deep colour and not too much alcohol. Other memory triggers of the Tempranillo are hints of plums and the texture of velvet. It is the backbone grape of good Rioja (does vanilla ring a bell?) and is also widely used in Spain's Penedès, Navarra and Valdepeñas. In Portugal it is used, too, in some Douro wines.

Cinsaut

Cinsaut is one of the frequent ingredients of the southern French cocktail for chunky reds along with Grenache, Carignan and in better wines, Syrah. It is a meaty chap, this, giving body and contributing softness, although not considered charming enough to make a wine anywhere in the world single-handedly; instead it contents itself with appearing on the list of ingredients of such wines as Châteauneuf-du-Pape, Côtes du Rhône, Côtes du Roussillon and so on.

Carignan

A surprisingly big volume producer in the south of the country, Carignan is the biggest red producer in France. It never gives its name to a wine and seldom performs on its own, but it's there, declared or not, in most reds of south-east France, producing inky dark wines, big and potentially tough (although modern techniques have done much to soften this tendency). A good cropper, it is found anonymously here and there in Italy and Spain and has been adopted with enthusiasm in California.

A Word or Two About Wine

 IN A LEGEND about how wine was first made, a neglected concubine in a harem in the Middle East decided to put an end to her life by drinking the juice from a jar marked 'poison'. It was actually simply the king's crafty hiding place for his best grapes, so marked to keep thieving fingers off. The grapes, however, had been left in the jar for rather too long on this occasion, had broken down, as old fruit will, into juice and pulp and undergone fermentation. So when the unhappy damsel removed the lid, she found something resembling poison in appearance and drank as much as she could. But instead of meeting her maker as she intended, a glow came to her cheeks and her spirits brightened considerably. She found her way instantly back into the king's affections – and grape juice left to work its magic in the royal amphoras replaced the firm, ripe berries as the favourite indulgence at court.

The discovery of how wine is made (or more precisely how it makes itself) could just as easily have taken place in your own kitchen, were you to be in the habit of leaving grapes in a jar. For wine is simply the fermented juice of grapes, and a bunch taken from the vine naturally harbours all the elements necessary for spontaneous fermentation.

Fermentation is the simple process whereby yeast converts sugar into alcohol (giving off carbon dioxide, incidentally, as a by-product, which simply escapes into the air unless trapped, as it is when making sparkling wine). Yeast is naturally present on the grape skin (the white bloom seen easily on black berries) and sugar is a major part of the pulp and juice. Hanging on the vine (and for that matter even sitting in your fruit bowl) these catalytic elements are kept apart by the skin, but crush the berries or leave them to moulder long enough for the skin to break down naturally, and on contact with each other, the tumultuous process will start. In ideal conditions, the hectic fermentation continues until either all the sugar has been converted into alcohol by the yeast, or until the alcohol level has become so high that it kills off any yeasts that remain.

If you were simply to stand back and let the grapes ferment themselves into wine without intervening in any way, though, it is extremely doubtful that the wine would be pleasant to drink. The wine-maker has to justify his existence somehow – and does so by engineering the perfect conditions, using the right raw materials, nowadays high tech equipment, and by manipulating the process to achieve the results he wants.

Different varieties of wine-making grapes are better suited to the geological and climatic conditions in different parts of the world, and using subtly different wine-making techniques, produce the infinite spectrum of flavours and styles of wine you find on the wine shop shelves. The juice of virtually all wine-making grapes is white; it is only the skins that are different in colour. So although to some extent the grapes themselves determine the style of the wine, it is critically the method used that dictates whether a wine is red, white or rosé, dry or sweet . . .

White wines may be made from grapes of either colour. If black grapes are used the skins are separated from the pulp as soon as possible to prevent them bleeding their colour into the juice. A wine made only from white grapes is sometimes called *blanc de blancs* in France (literally 'white of whites'), to distinguish it from a white wine including red grapes.

Red wine naturally depends for its colour on the pigment in the skins of dark grapes. Although white grapes may also occasionally be used in the blend, the dominant varieties must be black (or red as they are called in wine-making circles) to give enough colour. When making red wines, the skins are left in contact with the fermenting juice until sufficient colour has been extracted. Colour, however, is not the only gift of the red skins; tannin is another contribution they make to the wine, a valuable preserving agent (which incidentally gives a furry feeling to the inside of the cheeks and makes the mouth feel dry). If the wine is intended to be matured for a while before the cork is drawn, the tannin level may be high initially, but as the wine ages, it softens and blends in harmoniously with the other elements.

Wines made for early drinking are made in such a way that the tannin content is kept to a minimum. One method is *macération carbonique* which is used for making Beaujolais Nouveau and other juicy-fruity young wines. In this case the grapes are fermented uncrushed in whole bunches under pressure in sealed tanks, enzymes inside the skins doing the work of the yeasts. Concentration of fruit and elimination of tannin results.

Unless there is an amazing amount of sugar in the grapes (generally arising from the bunches of grapes being shrivelled up on the vine by the presence of a peculiar kind of highly prized mould on the skins which concentrates the juice), the yeasts will keep going until they have consumed all the sugar – so making dry wine. If the wine-maker wants to make an ordinary quality medium or sweet white wine out of unshrivelled grapes, he may either artificially halt the fermentation while some sugar still remains, or filter off all remaining yeasts at the end of the fermentation process and add sterilised grape juice to the wine.

Rosé wines are just what they seem to be; a halfway house between whites and reds. Their delicate shade is usually achieved by brief contact between the red grape skins and the juice, although some rosés (including most rosé Champagnes) are made by blending a little red wine into the white. As with red wines, contact with the skins imparts more than mere colour, it generally beefs up the wine, giving additional body and a stronger flavour.

Touching on the Slippery Slope

 JOKES ABOUT WINE – or more precisely about wine snobs – are almost as popular as the mother-in-law ones. Had wine been as much fancied by the Brits say fifty years ago as it is now, it would doubtless have been a regular music hall gag. All that 'you'll be amused by its presumption' nonsense would fit neatly into the song and dance routine. And to joke-crackers there's no subject matter more appealing than talk of slope and soil. It's considered quite preposterous that anyone in the world should claim to be able to spot the difference between one wine grown on one slope and another grown just down the road. But people can, and they do; quite simply because there are marked differences. It's not just a load of eyewash, I assure you.

Let me tell you why not. In common with most living things (ourselves included), grapes are largely water; getting on for 90 per cent of the berry is straightforward H_2O in fact. And where does the water come from? From the soil, of course, where it is sucked up by the plant's roots. It is quite possible for the soil in one particular vineyard to be quite different from that in another. And because the composition of the soil affects the water that permeates it, the soil in turn affects the precise taste of the wine.

If you look at a classic vine growing area in France, you'll see that vineyards are often interspersed with woods and fields. Now, because grapes in the best classified regions fetch a few bob, you can bet your life that any piece of land permitted to grow grapes will be regimented with rows of fecund vines. So you can therefore deduce that the plots covered by trees and grass are not legally designated fit for vine growing, because they have the wrong type of soil. If the soil were suitable, those areas, too, would be planted with the maximum number of vines allowed. Sometimes different soil types in the same area are allowed to support vines, in which case the more appropriate soil produces the better grapes to make the better wine.

So that takes care of ribald remarks about soil; not perhaps the most fascinating of subjects (which is why it merits only two paragraphs here) but an understandably vital one, especially to wine-makers. Climate and weather – and here the precise aspect of the slope comes in – are critical as well. Ideally the vine likes winters to be cold; cold enough to quash any growing activity during its resting period. From the spring, when the vine flowers, it's important to get enough sun, lasting through until after the harvest in the autumn. Enough but not too much; baking hot oven conditions produce wines that taste like cooked jam. No temperate fruit likes too much of a good thing; protracted growing seasons are best with the sun dished out consistently but cautiously.

The wine-producing regions of the world, therefore, lie in two bands around the globe, between 50° and 30° latitude in the north and between 30° and 50° latitude in the south. Technological discoveries have increasingly overcome natural disadvantages, and the quality of wines made in hot places (within these bands) is leaping forward all the time. However, generally speaking, the most propitious sites are the cooler ones. But there is then the worry of whether or not there will be enough sun. To make wine there must be adequate sugar in the grapes to create sufficient alcohol during fermentation and this sugar derives from the sun.

So wine-makers – or more precisely vine growers – setting their sights on producing nothing but the best, walk the tightrope between too much sun on the one hand and the perilous risk of too little on the other. This is where the precise slope becomes so important because it makes all the difference in a marginal growing area (England, Germany and Champagne are all very marginal growing areas for grapes) – the difference between catching the crucial rays and just missing them. The best site for a vineyard in a cool area, therefore, is a south-facing slope, sloping like a sunbather on a sunbed to catch the maximum number of each day's rays.

Wine is not simply a natural miracle (all those wondrous scents and flavours from a small, ordinary fruit), it's a scientific one as well. Everything that happens to the vine affects the ultimate taste of the wine; not merely the soil, climate and aspect, but the planting density of the vines, the pruning methods, the fertilisation, the water table and the rainfall. Don't nod off, I'm not going into all that here (or anywhere, come to that), just skirting round the edge . . . In the days of yore, the gnarled old peasant would tend his few rows in the way his ancestors had before, introducing, perhaps, one subtle twist in the procedure throughout a whole life devoted to the vine.

Innovation is rather quicker now, and the scene in vineyards around the world is rather less picturesque as a result, but not nearly so space age as some wineries. That's where the real technical revolution has taken place and 'everyday' (as opposed to extra-special occasion arm-and-a-leg jobs) wines are all the better for it, too. So let's get on with the tasting!

The
Best-known
Wines of the
World

France

FRANCE IS well up there with the largest producers of wine in the world and bags the largest share of the wine market in Britain. Let me boggle your minds with a couple of statistics. Each year, give or take the odd million bottles, about eight billion bottles of wine are produced in France, of which we consume about 287 million bottles. And that's only still table wine, leaving anything stronger or sparkling aside. Include them, and we're up to 320 million bottles a year.

But by no means is wine produced all over the country, far from it. It comes from individual regions scattered all over the place, but every single drop is somehow or other pigeon-holed. To help officials to keep tabs on all the producers, and more importantly on their precious products, every drop of wine is classified, both in terms of where it comes from and in terms of its quality. The most meagre quality made, called on the label just *Vin de Table* or table wine, is permitted to come from anywhere at all and its origins are not stated on the label. But every other drop has a declared provenance.

Another stupefying statistic coming up: there are (as far as I can count) about 777 different individual French wines, each governed by its own set of rules. Okay, so this doesn't strictly mean that there are 777 different areas. Sometimes wines from the same place but with a whisker of difference in quality will each have their own *appellations*, but that is the exception. So 777 isn't far off the number of completely different French wines that are produced, and a large number of them find their way to Britain and other countries to baffle customers perusing the wine shop shelves.

Now the reason that I am telling you all this is to introduce an excuse. I have to admit I have not written taste pictures of all the 777 different wines. Far from it. But what I have done is to concentrate on those that are most widely available in Britain through supermarkets and chains of high street wine shops. Because there is such an enormous variety of idiosyncratic wines out there on sale in the wine cellars of France, corporate wine buyers over here have a wide choice open to them. They all make sure that they have good supplies of all the most requested lines in their shops, but they also sometimes tickle our fancies with the odd obscure little *je ne sais quoi*. I've included what I consider to be the most fashionable of these idiosyncrasies (they come and they go) but in general I've concentrated on the old favourites, arranged according to the areas from which they come.

The French have been making wine since God was a boy. In the early days wine-makers, along with all the other inhabitants of each village, were very insular. They made their wine from the grape varieties that had been planted by their forebears and called the wine simply after the place where it was made. And that was good enough for them. The fact that it now leaves us with 777 different names to try to get to grips with is beside the point.

As a slightly more national approach began to be adopted, however, accepted standards of quality gradually began to be assumed for each wine. This century saw the formal ratification of all the various individual quality requirements for each named wine. To gain entitlement to the name by which wines from a particular place are known, a wine must satisfy these requirements. It then automatically also qualifies for the official quality status that goes with it. Essentially there are four bands of quality. But we don't get off quite as lightly in the 'names to remember' stakes as that might suggest, because within the top band there are many shapes of difference, as you'll see when you come to the section on Bordeaux.

As I've already mentioned, the lowliest quality status for French wine is *Vin de Table*. Because these are basically *mélanges* without any remarkable idiosyncrasies, usually being known simply by a brand name, none is included here. If you are wondering what has become of Piat d'Or and the like in *The Taste of Wine*, these are not candidates for inclusion because they are not individual wines; they are made up of blends of wines from anywhere in the country and do not depend on a consistent medley of grape varieties or anything as subtle as that. For the record, I personally think you would gain more satisfaction – and certainly get better value for money – from buying any one of the individual wines described between these covers than spending your money on an anonymous blend, no matter how the advertisements might try to persuade you otherwise. Let's get one thing straight; the French are in no position to *adore* Piat d'Or because it simply isn't available over there.

Vin de Pays, meaning simply country wine, is the next rung up the quality ladder after *Vin de Table*. Wines earning this title come from a declared area and must display the basic characteristics of wines from that area to qualify. Although in general *Vins de Pays* are ordinary quality plonks, there are also some delicious treats bearing this quality description on the label. If a wine-maker in a quality wine region elects to disregard the precise quality regulations (generally because he wants to grow grape varieties other than those specified), then his wine, no matter how brilliant it tastes, will be demoted to *Vin de Pays* status. This explains why you can sometimes have expensive looking bottles claiming to be simple *Vins de Pays*. For example in many areas of the south of France, classic grape varieties such as the Cabernet Sauvignon are barred from the list of permitted types, so any wine including this variety will be demoted in quality status.

Vin Délimité de Qualité Supérieure (simply think of VDQS) is an increasingly unusual classification covering the best of the 'ordinary' quality wines. Plonk with more knobs on, in effect. *Appellation Contrôlée* is the top-quality status for French wines, which range from merely good to the best that money can buy. When you see Appellation Contrôlée on the label of any French wine (bar Alsace), it will be associated with the name of a place, as in Appellation Bergerac Contrôlée. This shows that the wine satisfies the quality requirements specified for the precisely defined region of Bergerac.

Alsace

 LITTLE KNOWN and much underrated, wines from Alsace are named (unusually for France) after the grape varieties from which they are made. And you don't have to be an expert to recognise them at a glance – they come in distinctive extra-tall green flute bottles. These are straightforward 'purist' wines, faithfully mirroring the scents and flavours of the different types of grapes behind them; a godsend when confronted with a daunting wine list in a restaurant. In the 'Alsace' section (which may be feebly short, regrettably; these wines aren't very well known in Britain) you'll always know what you're getting – and it's likely to represent good value too; it's rare to find rip-offs and duds from Alsace.

There are six different white varieties in Alsace and one red: Riesling, Pinot Blanc, Pinot Gris (also known as Tokay d'Alsace), Sylvaner, Muscat and Gewürztraminer in the white corner, and Pinot Noir coping single-handedly in the red. Usually the varieties are used on their own although there are blends, known either simply as Vin d'Alsace, or Edelzwicker (but these are the least interesting wines from the area). Many of the names and some of the grape varieties are German, but don't be deceived, the style of wine-making is French and dry.

The Wines and Their Taste:

Gewürztraminer

This white is pungent, heady stuff, with perhaps the most distinctive character of any grape or wine, sweet and sour is how I describe Gewürztraminer. At first whiff, you're caught up in the rich, spicy scents of exotic fruits and scented soaps. It certainly seems sweet on the bouquet, but take a sip and you'll be surprised; it's not exactly sweet but instead, sweet-and-sour. Because it has bags of body and character, the wine appears richer and sweeter than it is; it is actually dry, with a kind of pungent taste, if you can imagine it, recalling

lychees and scented China teas. Being attractively peachy coloured, Gewürztraminer grapes give a golden tinge to the wine. They are also capable of producing high levels of alcohol, so watch out!

Appropriately, continuing in the Oriental vein, Gewürztraminers are a brilliant choice to accompany Chinese and Eastern food. Some are comparative heavyweights among whites, a bit of a mouthful to tackle without grub (although fine with all the exotic flavours Chinese food can conjure up); others are more delicate and floral and are also good – and unusual – chilled well and sipped on their own.

Muscat

You'd imagine *all* wines would be grapey, wouldn't you? But when you look more closely, you'll find very few actually are – except those made from the Muscat. Many Muscats are grapey and sweet; in Alsace, true to style, these white wines are grapey and dry, a marvellously mouth-filling combination – plenty of body and a bit of spice, too (I hope no-one ever says that of me). Quite like the Gewürztraminer in style, though less so.

Pinot Blanc

Although the Pinot Blanc is seldom much to write home about, its wines are deliciously simple and do have an enjoyable creaminess to them, an appley, grassy quality mingled in with a spritely lemony edge – fond reminiscence for me of *citron pressé* (you know, fresh lemon, sugar and water). There's not usually much of a bouquet to this wine, but have a swig and you may find a faintly lavendery quality; a touch of honey and a pinch of spice or the merest suggestion of Parma violet sweets. Chill it down and then drink it down, that's my advice!

Pinot Gris or Tokay d'Alsace

Spice is the first thing this delicious (and sadly rather rare) white wine reminds you of; a kind of spicy nut roast with vague hints of sandalwood. You may also get a faint breeze of damp moss on the bouquet, too. Into the taste, and you find more ripeness, depth and breadth than in other Alsace wines

Major wine-growing areas

and a soft, caressing texture. Although dry, there's a sense of sweetness reminiscent of shortbread biscuits sprinkled with cinnamon and just the merest suggestion of pears. A lovely mind-focusing glass to enjoy before food, or with slightly spicy (though not too heavy) dishes such as vegetable casseroles and pies.

Pinot Noir

In Alsace, Burgundy's top red grape produces lively, light – so light they almost verge on being rosé, sometimes with a rusty tinge – reds with an unusual pungence to them. You'll notice the sweet scent of cherries or maybe strawberries and a reticent fruitiness in the taste, too. It can sometimes seem the fruit has been picked and crushed with the leaves, giving a 'green' tinge to the taste, almost an unripeness, but this is offset by a vibrance, a liveliness and a sense of youth. The light styles are as good served slightly chilled as they are at the traditional room temperature.

Riesling

Recognise the name? It's Germany's number one grape (known also as Rhine Riesling and Johannisberg Riesling) but here, and only here, it's 100 per cent French. (Such is French paranoia about rival wine-makers that planting of the essentially German Riesling grape is forbidden more than thirty miles into France; Alsace just sneaks into this band.)

In Alsace this bone dry – as dry as you can imagine – white wine shows all this aristocratic grape variety has to show, unmasked by sweetness. Young Riesling has the scent of alpine flowers, hauntingly delicate and scented with a streamlined purity; sharp but elusive. As the wine matures, it takes on that characteristic (of the Riesling, that is) petrolly note – like an aeroplane revving up – and a waft of honey. On the taste, the floweriness persists, and the petrol, giving almost an oily feel.

Very occasionally, the wines are made in a sweeter style, in which case the label will declare *vendange tardive* (meaning late picked, when the grapes had built up enormous reserves of sugar), or *sélection de grains nobles*. But generally Alsace Rieslings are steely and dry and make good rapiers to cut through bland food . . . because of their delicacy, it is a mistake to match them with anything too strong, as powerful flavours would drown them out – fish is fine.

Sylvaner

Another favourite German variety, Sylvaner crosses the border into Alsace to make slightly bland white wine. On the bouquet you'll find hints of new mown hay plus the biscuity notes of crumbled digestives; like the base for a cheesecake. The hay connotations continue into the taste, silky in feel though rather nondescript in flavour. There can be resinous associations and soft icing sugar sweetness to counterbalance the acidity. A 'safe' wine to serve to a mixed group, it couldn't possibly offend anyone.

Bordeaux

 WITHOUT DOUBT this is the most famous wine area in the world. And if the name doesn't mean anything to you – how about claret? For this is where it comes from, every single drop of it from the £100 000 bottles (phantasmagorical prices are frequently fetched by great, old claret at auction) to the accessibly priced ordinary claret on every off-licence and supermarket shelf. Confined within the Gironde *département* around the estuary and rivers of the Dordogne and the Garonne, some 250 000 acres lend themselves to vines bent on producing an astonishing 530 million or so bottles each year.

The suitability of the soil and the climate for encouraging wine-making grapes to perform at their optimum is the main reason for Bordeaux's marvellous track record. There are some sites within the region that are considered almost perfect for producing certain types of wine, whether they be marvellously complex reds or impossibly delicious dessert wines. Nature contributes her share to Bordeaux's greatness. But so, too, do the British, in their own small way, because it was during the three hundred years that Bordeaux belonged to Britain (it came with Eleanor of Aquitaine's dowry when she married Henry II in 1152 and was lost again at the end of the 100 years war in 1453) that the export of the wines began to flourish and their fame was first established and then spread. The Bordeaux wine trade still has an English flavour, and many of the châteaux have very English names, such as Palmer, Brown, Clarke and Haut-Brion (O'Brien?).

Although Bordeaux is synonymous with illustrious châteaux responsible for hand-crafting wines destined to make sommeliers bow and customers gasp, only a tiny proportion of the wine produced, in fact, commands such adulation. Okay, so the lesser wines are in general pretty all right in their own way, too, but not every bottle of Bordeaux wine is a masterpiece; countless average and even run-of-the-mill offerings leave the busy commercial town and port of the same name each year boasting the Bordeaux *appellation* on the label, and must then fight wines with less lustrous names for a place in the customer's shopping bag.

Understanding how the *Appellation Contrôlée* system works in Bordeaux is the key to knowing what to expect from any given bottle. Remember *Appellation Contrôlée* actually means that the use of the place name is 'controlled', permitting only those wines meeting the standards set for that particular place or *appellation* to use it. The broad rule is that the larger the area 'controlled' by the *appellation*, the humbler will be the wine. Any wine made in any one of the 250 000 designated acres is entitled to the most basic *appellation*, which is Appellation Bordeaux Contrôlée, and this will appear on the label. Don't forget, the name Bordeaux – even with a fancy-sounding château name attached – is not a synonym for excellence; among those thousands of acres are some less propitious ones, and some that are less well managed, too. Some wine-makers are a lot better at their job than others, but come what may, *all* can call themselves members of the same AC Bordeaux club. Bordeaux Supérieur (and this, too, has its own *appellation*) means the wine has naturally achieved more alcohol (because the grapes were that much sweeter when they were picked).

The huge Bordeaux region is divided into smaller defined areas with well-known names such as Médoc, Graves, St-Emilion and Entre-Deux-Mers, each producing wines in a certain style and entitled to their own *appellation*. Wines entitled to this more precise *appellation* will certainly take it, showing that they are further up the quality ladder. Areas such as Médoc are then subdivided again into the Médoc, and the generally superior, more southerly Haut-Médoc. The Haut-Médoc (which, of course, has its own *appellation*) is then subdivided into parishes or communes, again with their own AC. So Margaux is a commune within the Haut-Médoc (and you can bet your life that any wine permitted to put Appellation Margaux Contrôlée on the label will do so, as opposed to going under the name Haut-Médoc, Bordeaux Supérieur or Bordeaux . . . it's a handle worth having).

Spiralling into even dizzier echelons, the top châteaux (classified in 1855) will declare themselves to be *Cru Classé* on the label; if they are magnificently special, *Premier Cru* or *Premier Grand Cru Classé*. The wines of St-Emilion have a slightly different and less specific rating system, whereby châteaux wines will be either *Grand Cru*, or the better ones, *Grand Cru Classé* and the top, *Premier Grand Cru Classé*. Because this book is essentially about widely available (and affordable) wines, I will not be dwelling long on this narrowly available and thoroughly unaffordable plane.

So, the wines of Bordeaux (which cover almost all styles, the red clarets, dry whites, sweet whites and rosés) present themselves in a number of ways. Starting from the bottom, there are 'ordinary' clarets and white wines, named either simply that (Claret or Bordeaux Blanc) or known by brand names (such as Mouton Cadet); they may be called simply by their regional names (Médoc, St-Emilion, etc.); or they may be named after individual châteaux. This is the tricky bit, because there are about 7000 of these . . . The only hope you have of knowing or predicting what's what is by looking at the *appellation*; just remember, the larger the area described by the *appellation*, the more ordinary will be the wine. So, you have châteaux that are simple Appellation Bordeaux Contrôlée, you have châteaux with an *appellation* of an area, such as Médoc; of a commune, such as Margaux. And as the *appellation* becomes more specific, so you can expect more noughts to add themselves to the price.

The backbone grapes of red claret are Cabernet Sauvignon, Cabernet Franc and Merlot, although you'll never see these declared on the label. In the days when Bordeaux wines first became important and acquired their own names, it was the place that was considered the crucial information to put on the label (regardless of the grape varieties). Now the fashion is for grapes to lead on labels of comparatively 'new wines', often being single-handedly responsible for a particular wine. That's not the Bordeaux way at all. In Bordeaux the blend is the thing; the careful orchestration of wines from different grapes, combined to make a complete, balanced whole. Generally speaking, the Cabernet Sauvignon dominates the blend in the Médoc, the Merlot in St-Emilion and Pomerol.

Principal white grape varieties are Sémillon and Sauvignon, which are used for both dry and sweet wines (with occasionally a little Muscadelle added). The Sauvignon content is generally increasing in dry wines – and may even make up 100 per cent; if so, it'll probably say so on the label.

Each of the areas within the catchment of Bordeaux has its own subtle characteristics. And so I will describe those of the wines most commonly available.

The Wines and Their Taste:

Bordeaux Blanc

This used certainly to be a name to avoid on the label if you didn't want a glass of something rather flabby and sickly; but things are looking up. 'New technology' has come to the rescue, streamlining the wines and cleaning them up. Watch out the Loire! White Bordeaux is snapping at your heels, offering excellent alternatives, often at better prices. Bordeaux Blanc can come from anywhere across Bordeaux's undulating plains, and is the name by necessity taken on by the region's curiosities, such as *dry* wines from Sauternes, and white wines from great red Bordeaux châteaux.

Bordeaux Blanc as a name covers many styles – sweet, medium, medium dry – but you'll always find a little honeyed sweetness in there, a little waxiness from the Sémillon. If you want something drier, go for Bordeaux Sec, which means there is more astringent Sauvignon Blanc in the cocktail, giving a touch more citrus acidity. Or for something seriously dry, try Bordeaux Sauvignon, which has to be 100 per cent Sauvignon Blanc and can be raspingly dry with that characteristic unripe gooseberry smack you expect from this grape. The examples from Bordeaux are among the most aggressive Sauvignons you'll find, a shock if you're not expecting it, but a great pleasure when served well chilled in high summer.

Bordeaux Rouge

Can be called just that on the label, or 'Claret' (seeing the word claret on the label points to a pretty junior wine, fine claret never declares itself as such), or even under a château name (with the Appellation Bordeaux Contrôlée classification listed earlier). But call itself what it will, this is ordinary red Bordeaux from anywhere in the area, made from a mix of the three red grape types Cabernet Sauvignon, Cabernet Franc and Merlot. Quality and style vary quite a bit – don't expect too great an insight into great red Bordeaux from this humble rung of the ladder. But there are some typical wines nonetheless. Price and quality go pretty much hand in hand; the cheaper the wine, the sooner it should be drunk is the rule.

Typical scents held in a glass of this stuff are the inside of a cigar box, freshly cut wood and herbaceous borders, but don't be disappointed if they don't exactly spring out. To taste, the wine seems actively dry – drying in the mouth, too, and a little abrasive with sharp edges. Fruit, when you find it, is a blessing; generally the smoother, sweeter, fleshier wines are heavy on the Merlot grape. Bordeaux Supérieurs – with their half degree more alcohol, derived from the grapes being that much riper at harvest time – tend to be fractionally riper and smoother, packing in (if you're lucky) a greater punch of characteristic blackcurranty fruit flavours.

Entre-Deux-Mers

The name means literally 'between two seas'; the 'seas' in question being the Rivers Dordogne and Garonne between which the wedge of land bearing this *appellation* sits. Entre-Deux-Mers, with its old-fashioned labels bearing plates of seafood, used to be a white wine to avoid at (almost) all costs, being lifeless, cloying and dull. Now it's better known as the home of cleaner, drier medleys made from the same grapes (Sauvignon with some Sémillon) but in the squeaky clean new style. The reds from the area fall into the simple Bourgogne Rouge category.

Cut grass, that's what the best examples conjure up, tinged with the inevitable goosegog flavours associated with the Sauvignon. They should be cracked open as young as possible and then act like a squeeze of lemon with a plate of seafood, adding a rapier thrust to rich oily fish.

Graves

Bordeaux city is on the move, south into the ancient Graves wine region. Look on the map and you'll think there's room enough for everyone, but the best wines come from the gravelly soils (hence the name) close to the city in the north of the district where Bordeaux's property giants have set their sites. Further south, less propitious sand and clay soils dominate, but there is lots of sun there, contributing a silky roundness to the wines. The reds are the giants, with whites cowering in the background – with just cause in the sweet and soupy past, but now there are some stylish white Graves to bring honour back to the name. A new *appellation*, Pessac-Léognan, now encompasses the best communes. Look for it on the label for the best wines.

Red **There are rose-tinted scents to these firm, bricky, almost earthy clarets hiding behind their silky smooth exterior. At best, they positively burst with ripe fruit, the sun giving a roasted raisiny feel and conjuring up visions of autumn bonfires. Some are still a bit too trad for their own good, being a touch on the tough and tannic side, though.**

White **White Graves are a cut above ordinary Bordeaux Sec, in the main. Look out for ripe apricot flavours spiked by fresh acidity and the spicy suggestion of smoky oak. Graves Supérieurs have a slightly sweeter edge to them, linked to marginally higher alcohol content caused by riper fruit.**

Margaux

The red jewel in the Médoc's crown, Margaux, harbours more top flight châteaux – including Château Margaux, of course – than any other area of Bordeaux. Wines simply called Margaux, though, have nothing to do with the premier château of the same name, they simply come from within the same commune. At best these are lesser shadows of the great wine; at worst, disappointingly sludgy and nebulous.

Scents that have been known to fly out of a glass of Margaux include violets, nutmeg, wet blossom, roasted coffee beans – plus, of course, concentrated blackcurrants and a hint of plums. This is what is described as 'elegant' claret; beautifully brought up and perfectly mannered with no harsh edges or awkward corners.

Médoc

Here flourish most of the dizzily famous names of Bordeaux, though generally in the southern reaches of the Haut-Médoc. The northern bit is a good source of smooth easy drinkers – much like ordinary Bordeaux Rouge, but with knobs on; meaning they are finer, fruitier and altogether juicier.

Fleshy around the middle is how you might describe a good Médoc, with herby scents and a wet watercressy edge to them. But there's always a good prod of acidity, even a hint of mint, to dig the fleshy fruit in the ribs.

Premières Côtes de Bordeaux

A narrow strip of land on the right (you could say wrong) bank of the River Garonne opposite Bordeaux, this region produces both red and white wines, the best of which have the name of an individual commune tagged on to the end of the name, such as Premières Côtes de Bordeaux-Cadillac. It is legitimate for the communes to stand on their own on the label, too. Reds, with family resemblances to the Graves across the river, are improving all the time. Whites tend to be sweet . . . and as a consequence, rather unfashionable. Some growers are following the dry-as-a-bone trend, but then they have to give up the Premières Côtes de Bordeaux name and call their wines simply Bordeaux Sec.

Premières Côtes de Bordeaux Blanc are simple semi-sweet wines, sometimes freshly so, though unfortunately they can sometimes be rather cloying with a catch in the throat. Three of the best communes giving their names to their wines are Cadillac, Loupiac and Ste-Croix-du-Mont.

Cadillac The ugly mould responsible for making Sauternes hum with honeyed brilliance, sporadically visits the vines of Cadillac, so their sweetness is much less intense and rich. They tend to be lightly (and admittedly a bit boringly) sweet as opposed to luscious.

Loupiac A richer and more thrusting wine, this is the top Premières Côtes de Bordeaux.

Ste-Croix-du-Mont Golden, waxy and oily from the slithery Sémillon grape, honeyed, but still a long way behind Sauternes in brilliance.

St-Emilion

A pretty hilltop village gives its name to Merlot-dominated clarets from hundreds of small properties dotted across its 'côte' or hillside. Grand Cru is liberally splashed across the label of St-Emilions, but has less meaning here than elsewhere. Grand Cru *Classé*, however, means the wine is genuinely superior, with Premier Grand Cru Classé putting the wine in the absolute top class. Simple St-Emilions are often surplus wine from the châteaux and can represent very good buys.

The red claret for the white wine drinker, this tends to be easier drinking and more generous than most. The Merlot grape contributes a velvety softness to the wine which can put you in mind of Dundee cake with its toffee-like fruitiness. The second most important grape variety in St-Emilion is Cabernet Franc, which adds a faint grassiness and a peppery twist on the finish.

St-Estèphe

A northerly outpost on the Garonne's left bank, tending to be more down-to-earth and tougher than the string of glories farther south. More Merlot is being introduced to soften the style of this red.

When young, St-Estèphes tend to be hard, tannic and mouth-puckering, leaving a stalky, grassy feeling in the mouth. Given time, though, the dry toughness softens revealing curranty fruit.

Burgundy

 A MAGICAL NAME to wine lovers around the world, Burgundy is acknowledged to be the holy grail of Pinot Noir and Chardonnay, two of the world's most important grapes. The region, running from north to south roughly from Champagne to the Rhône, puts out arguably the best dry white wines and some of the best reticent reds in the world. Conditions on the bosomy hills and in the pastoral villages running south-west down from Dijon are perfect for producing the highly complex, subtle, finely tuned wines most enjoyed by 'connoisseurs' with their finely tuned palates. The best known Burgundian white wine, Chablis, comes from its own separate sateilite area at 10 o'clock to the rest of the region and sixty miles south-east of Paris. Beaujolais (for know it or not, Beaujolais is recognised as part of Burgundy) is to the south, between Mâcon and Lyon.

Don't expect a true Burgundy, red or white (we'll leave Beaujolais on one side for the moment) to jump out of the glass at you and boast of its brilliance. Burgundies are not boasters; in fact by comparison with their equivalents from Australia, they are positively shy in virtually all respects, bar their prices. It's the old supply and demand equation. Burgundy produces a fraction of the fine wine put out by France's other great wine area, Bordeaux, and because her progeny are so highly rated and consequently so highly sought after, she can charge for them what she will.

Although great Burgundy is undeniably formidably great, lesser examples bearing the 'Bourgogne' name can be sadly disappointing – and over-priced to boot. In common with every other wine-producing region in the world, Burgundy has her high spots and her low. But she also has a system of classifying her wines in terms of their quality, which is a help if you can get to grips with it. At the bottom of the hierarchy sit two ordinary reds, the (despite its name, not very grand) Bourgogne Grand Ordinaire and Bourgogne Passe-Tout-Grains.

The exclusive grape variety for all fine red Burgundies is Pinot Noir, but in the lower echelons of the quality scale, Gamay (the Beaujolais grape, of course) is likely to reign instead. Next up the ladder come Appellations Bourgognes Contrôlées, rouge and blanc, a general classification covering wines in all parts of the region. Chardonnay is the only white grape permitted in most Burgundy *appellations,* but there is an exception, Bourgogne Aligoté, a grape which always carries its own *appellation* no matter where in the region it comes from.

Moving up from the bottom rung of the quality ladder, wines from collections of specific villages may go into a *Villages* catch-all, such as Côte de Beaune-Villages. When a specific *Village* is named, this means the wine is another rung up the quality ladder. A village name attached to a vineyard name (probably hyphenated together) in letters of equal size (important, this) is superior quality again; very superior, in fact, being of Premier Cru status. If the lettering for the vineyard name is much smaller than that of the village name, however, drop back one rung of the quality ladder. This is not a Premier Cru wine.

Top whack Burgundies, wines from the absolute best vineyards, are called Grands Crus, and are so special they go by their vineyard name alone; so you have Le Montrachet, a Grand Cru, and Puligny-Montrachet (Puligny being the village, Montrachet, the best vineyard) being a Premier Cru. Being French, though, and giving huge priority to anything gastronomic, in everyday life the village likes to go by the name Puligny-Montrachet because it is so proud of its best vineyard.

Largely because of France's inheritance laws, which insist on the division and distribution of the property equally among the sons on death, Burgundy's vineyards may be divided between tens or even hundreds of owners, so if you are really going to *know* Burgundy, you have to start by programming your brain to remember scores of names, not just the names of the slopes and the villages and the vineyards, but of the owners of the various pockets of the vineyards, and of the merchants who buy from the individual growers and sell the wine under their own name.

If you merely want to enjoy an affordable glass, however, you can relax. There are plenty of wine lovers around (myself included) who are happy to admit they don't really *know* Burgundy. But, like me, too, they probably know what they like. Here are some insights into the wines behind the labels most frequently seen on supermarket and high street off-licence shelves.

The Wines and Their Taste:

Bourgogne Aligoté

Aligoté is the 'other' white Burgundy grape, now so over-shadowed by Chardonnay that it is gradually disappearing from our shelves . . . and from the vineyards of Burgundy. Because they have their own *appellation*, Bourgogne Aligoté, which is always prominent on the label, these individually tart white wines are easily spotted on the shelves.

The Aligoté is a tricky, tart grape, which at its best has attractive floral associations and a slight whiff of vanilla. The best examples come from Bouzeron and will say so on the label, and these are silkier and less abrasive than many. Classically in Burgundy this wine is the base for Kir: a dash of the blackcurrant liqueur, crème de cassis, in the

bottom of the glass topped up with Bourgogne Aligoté, they are the perfect match for each other.

Bourgogne Blanc

Chardonnay is the most important grape behind this ordinary white Burgundy, although the Pinot Blanc is allowed in, too. This is a basic quality classification, but it can sometimes harbour some good wines, minor mirrors to the great treats that have made the name famous . . . if you're lucky.

Coming from anywhere in the large and varied catchment area, there can be a subtle variety of styles, from the taut, tart style of the Yonne and the north, through the nutty, creamy flavours of the peachy Côte d'Or in the middle, to the appley, chalky flavours of the south. Wood-ageing makes a big difference (it may say *élevé en fût* on the label), adding a depth and breadth and a perceptible vanilla tang.

Bourgogne Passe-Tout-Grains

The humblest red Burgundy you're likely to encounter in Britain, this is a good buy to look out for. It's a blend of Gamay (dominating) with Pinot Noir and makes a good, light, juicy-fruity blend.

As light in colour as you can get in a red wine, this lightness suggests what to expect when you take a gulp. The first characteristic to hit you is that this wine has a sharp sting to it, swinging through the jammy layers of young fruit. As it begins to mature, the fragrant, fleshy fruits of the Pinot Noir peg on strawberry nuances and the merest hint of plum jam. A good way to serve it is chilled (like Beaujolais) in summer, when it can take on not merely the trad dishes you associate with red wine but fish, too. Try it with trout or mackerel, something with substance and character of its own.

Bourgogne Rouge

Red wines from the whole Burgundian region from way up in Chablis country down to Beaujolais can take this name, which in effect gathers up the misfits which have no other category to call their own. So there are some pretty disappointing offerings mixed in with the good. In the far north, the less lustrous César and Tressot grapes may be used;

Chablis	Côte Chalonnaise
Côte de Nuits	Mâcon
Côte de Beaune	Beaujolais

the Pinot Noir accounts for the Bourgognes Rouges from the major central area; with the Gamay making some examples in Mâcon and Beaujolais country. If the Pinot Noir is behind the label, you can bet it'll be *on* the label too, so that's one way to look out for classic quality.

Because the Pinot Noir is an awkward, tempestuous little ripener, you can find some lily-livered, watery sweet examples, regrettably, but the model they should all be striving to emulate is packed with summer-pudding fruits heralded by a wet strawberry/cherry-like bouquet. Gamay-led Bourgognes Rouges (which are the exceptions) are piercing and have a 'newly-picked' feel to them.

Chablis

A tricky one, Chablis. Of course this large independent area of Burgundy is capable of producing marvellous restrained Chardonnays, or it would never have become so famous in the first place. But its fame, coupled with its easy-to-pronounce name, means that it has been put about altogether too liberally for its own good. Chablis is a must on any self-respecting wine shelf. But buying good Chablis to put on the wine shelf in the first place is a very vexing business. Chablis growers, like all fine Burgundy growers, need to establish long-standing relationships with their customers; they don't – and in most cases bar the co-operative can't – just hand over huge volumes of the right white wine at the right price. So I'm afraid I cannot recommend supermarkets and high street wine chains as sources of good Chablis. They have it, certainly, but it ain't necessarily good. Go instead to an independent wine merchant who can buy small parcels of what he really likes.

Wines called plain, straight Chablis are the most dodgy in this class. They should be cautious Chardonnay with restrained buttery, unripe banana and custard flavours, but more often they seem like a light, sharp, mean and green white wine that has been strained through a doormat – and for that you pay a hefty price. To purchase Chablis with a greater chance of being remarkable, you have to look for Premier Cru wines which cost at least a couple of pounds more. Then you'll have a glimpse of what made this name famous: delicate pineapple and apricot scents mingled with vanilla, leading you into a smooth, coaxing, complete,

succulently restrained taste. Grand Cru wines are the best and by far the most expensive of all.

Côte de Beaune-Villages

Sixteen of the individual Beaune villages are allowed to use this name for their red wine, although they seldom do, because they also have their own village name to go under. However, there are exceptional circumstances and *négociants* buy up parcels of wine and blend them to make this respectable *appellation*. Chanson is a good name to look out for.

In their youth, these wines can be a bit tough and tannic, but they smooth out with time (three years or so) to give the characteristic cherry edge with a slug of vegetable scent and flavour married in.

Côte Chalonnaise

Geographically, this range of hills is an extension of the illustrious Côtes d'Or (see opposite) and the wines are recommendable affordable versions. They are affordable partly because they are lesser wines, but more importantly because the area suffered various knocks this century and has only just got itself up and running again, so it hasn't yet acquired the fame that inevitably bumps up prices. You won't find the Côte name on the label, but instead one of three *appellations* tidily offering a selection of red and white wines. (There is a fourth, Givry, but it is little seen in Britain.)

Rully At the top end of the Côte Chalonnaise, Rully is the nearest neighbour to the Côtes de Beaune – and nearest in style. Red and white wine are made in about equal proportions. There is a fatness and ripeness to the red which is reminiscent of strawberries and vegetable compost at the same time (a better marriage than it may seem). Look, too, for a rusty, ferrous note in there. Despite the ripeness, the overall impression, however, is light and slight. The whites are serious white Burgundies with scents of peach and apricot, rounded off by vanilla if the wine has been aged in wood. There's a *pain grillé* edge, too, as they'd call it in France, toasty to the likes of you and me. You get more concentration of flavour from this *appellation* than from the others of the Côte Chalonnaise.

Mercurey Going south, the second *appellation* concentrates on good value reds with a surprising punch of acidity which can slightly upset the cherry cart . . . for cherry is the fruit this wine most easily calls to mind. Definitely food wine – go for a good substantial roast, plainly done, to get the best partnership. The white can be heavy, full-flavoured wine leaving a lasting taste impression in the mouth. Typical Chardonnay, it has a slight taste of limes without the associated tartness. Versions aged in wood definitely need food such as chicken in a rich creamy sauce or strongly flavoured fish such as turbot or bass.

Montagny All white wines here, are called Premiers Cru unless proved otherwise (by failing to have enough sugar in the grapes at harvest time). Summer-ripe fruit is instantly noticeable when you get your nose in the glass, fleetingly peachy with a little hint of cinnamon. There's a steely edge, too, in this clean, cool wine, allowing the subtle fragrance to show through. There can be a slight liveliness on the tongue and a finish verging on the sweet.

Côte d'Or

You'll never actually find this golden name on the label, the 'Golden Hillside', so called, is the heart of Burgundy, producing the finest red and white wines the area – and some would say the world – can do. The best wines are known by either their vineyard or their village name and, hardly surprisingly, they don't come cheap. I'm not listing these individual gems here on the pretext that there's no place for a treatise on the crown jewels in a branch of a high street jewellery chain. But just as the sort of jewellery most of us may occasionally buy, loosely resembles the royal baubles in their own modest way so, too, do the individual wines described in this section reflect some of the glories of great and wonderfully expensive – too expensive for our purposes – red and white Burgundy.

Hautes-Côtes de Beaune

The higher slopes and plateaux behind the famed slopes responsible for putting out Burgundy's greatest wines have their own more modest *appellation*; and their own enthusiastic wine-makers hell-bent on showing the big boys a thing or two.

The reds from the Pinot Noir tend to be on the light side (not much wrong with that) but still give you those strawberry patch aromas, tinged by a tougher earthier edge with a firm lash of acidity to whip them into shape. If you can find them at the right price, these are good approachable introductions to the all-time greats. Little white is seen here.

Hautes-Côtes de Nuits

This *appellation* covers the fourteen villages hidden in the hills behind the famous Nuits slopes, where the weather and crops are more rugged and less consistent. But in good sunny years, these hidden vineyards can throw out some well-priced red treats.

Vibrantly fruity, lively and refreshing, the reds are a shade lighter than those from the Hautes-Côtes de Beaune. Again the Chardonnay whites are hardly seen here.

Mâcon Rouge

Going south from what we think of as Burgundy proper, on the way to Beaujolais, there are the calmly undulating hills of the Mâcon area, punctuated by pretty Romanesque villages. From these old-world pastures come light, straightforward reds made from Beaujolais's Gamay grape, although this is predominantly a white wine area.

You'll find the fresh, enticing scent of red berry fruits coming off these wines – redcurrants, blackcurrants and raspberries – tinged with a touch of spice. They are like Beaujolais, really, although less so; generally less vibrant and zingy than offerings from further south. Mâcon Rouge benefits from being chilled, when it makes a good summer glugger. Good food partners are pork, ham and duck.

Mâcon-Blanc Villages

This is another foxy little *appellation* designed, seemingly, to catch us out. Here the name Mâcon is linked to that of any one of 43 village names, get it? You actually need hoist on board only a small handful such as Lugny, Viré and Chardonnay (yes, a village as well as a grape, to add to the confusion).

Anyway these are all Chardonnay wines best tackled young when they have a slight apple and apple blossom character.

Pouilly-Fuissé

Not a great buy, this, so I will be brief. It is an over-hyped Chardonnay from the Mâconnais, much fancied in America (hence an unjustified price boom). Not to be confused with Pouilly-Fumé from the Loire which is made from Sauvignon Blanc.

The steely, crisp and dry character almost suppresses the juicy, creamy fruits bouncing to get out. The best examples are oak-aged, contributing powerful vanilla flavours touched by hints of hazelnuts and roasted almonds.

St-Véran

From way down on the border of Beaujolais country, directly south of Pouilly-Fuissé, St-Véran produces finely honed Chardonnays *à la* Pouilly-Fuissé, but at a smidgen of the price; these whites are some of southern Burgundy's best buys.

Dry, fragrant wines with lemony-honeyed hints. In their infancy, they smell of peaches, pears and cream, and as they age, they take on sedate honeysuckle and broom notes with a good whiff of almonds, honey and gunflint. Oysters would be a classic companion, or other exotic or commonplace shellfish.

Beaujolais

 BEAUJOLAIS IS wine of incomparable hype, particularly in the silly season of November when the Nouveau first comes on stream. Beaujolais is legally a satellite of Burgundy, but producing very different wines, the reds all from the Gamay grape, which reaches its crescendo of potential in the pretty 'Clochemerle' villages running north–south from Mâcon to Lyon. There is a clearly defined family tree of quality among reds (accounting for most Beaujolais). At the bottom are wines simply called Beaujolais. Now more than 50 per cent of these are produced as *Nouveaux*, that is (frequently suicidally) young, being offered for sale only a month or so after the harvest.

Climbing in quality you find wines called Beaujolais-Villages, coming from those villages deemed to have the right conditions for making better wine. Top of the tree are the *Crus*, wines named after any one of ten individual villages. Then there are the (few) rosés, paler – frequently downright pallid – forms of the reds, and white Beaujolais made from the Chardonnay grape.

The Wines and Their Taste:

Beaujolais Nouveau or Primeur

When the new Beaujolais first hits the bars and shelves in Britain on the third Thursday of November each year, it reveals itself to you, warts and all; there's been no time for the wine to soften with time or for the 'faults' to dim. In a good year (that means a consistently warm one), the purply bright wine that splashes into your glass has a fresh, come-onish juicy-fruitiness to it. You can smell soft, squashy summer fruits in there, a hint of rubber and the slight tang of cheesy feet. Don't be put off, they all work well together, particularly if the fruit dominates. The acidity is apparent in a tart, fizz-on-the-tongue sort of way and the overall impression is of a wine that is joyously light. In less propitious years, the acidity rules, the fruit is mean and the overall impression is sharp and tart. As the days and weeks go by, though, the wine has a chance to get itself together and tasted a month or so after the release date could be surprisingly improved. It's supposed to be over and done with by Easter, but good Nouveau can taste good until the next juvenile batch becomes available; it's disappeared from the off-licence shelves by then, so you'll have to buy your stocks to keep for yourself. Definitely serve all Nouveau chilled.

Beaujolais

Wines called simply Beaujolais are, in effect, just maturer versions of Beaujolais Nouveau, but with Nouveau being such a marketing wizz, most of the best bog-standard Beaujolais is now made as Nouveau, leaving rather disappointing red wines to fly the flag for ordinary Beaujolais.

High street wines called simply Beaujolais can be extremely dreary, lacking the jammy fruit, the bright, exciting verve you might hope for. Dull Beaujolais is uncompromisingly dull; never pretending to be anything other than an instantly appealing glassful – without the instant appeal, there ain't much else. One further word of warning:

Beaujolais &
Beaujolais-
Villages

Beaujolais Crus: Chiroubles

St-Amour   Morgon

Juliénas   Regnié

Chénas   Brouilly

Moulin-à-Vent   Côte de Brouilly

Fleurie

if they start tired, these Beaujolais will totally have run out of puff by the June following the harvest (indicated by the date on the label). If you want a Beaujolais in the summer, buy a Beaujolais-Villages, or a *Cru* instead.

Beaujolais-Villages

Better quality than ordinary Beaujolais, and considerably cheaper than the *Cru* wines named after individual villages, this class represents the best value for money. With all the elements working well together, this slightly heavier, richer red wine can recall the smell of gym shoes running on a hot road – honestly, get your nose in a glass and see what I mean. Being a bit more robust, this wine can be served at room temperature. You should still be drinking it in the year following the harvest, or at most into its second summer. After that, it will be starting to go downhill.

Cru Beaujolais

The best the area can produce with subtle differences between the individual villages, which are, working from north to south:

Saint-Amour The romantic name (and small production) of this wine puts on it a price premium – which can sometimes be worth it for the softness, almost voluptuousness, you find from this intense Beaujolais. Don't drink it too young (two to three years old).

Juliénas A little firmer than the norm, Juliénas has a full-blown gym shoe flavour.

Moulin-à-Vent The fullest bodied Beaujolais, characterised by an earthiness in the taste, this wine ages well and becomes gradually more like a Pinot Noir Burgundy. On a restaurant wine list where all the vintages look suspiciously old (curiously many restaurateurs haven't yet twigged that almost all Beaujolais is best drunk young), go for Moulin-à-Vent.

Chénas Chénas is seldom found, but when you do, expect it to be light and spritely when young, with more the weight of a Burgundy as it ages.

Fleurie Best known, best liked and most outrageously priced of the *Crus*, good Fleurie (and regrettably not all of it is) conveniently lives up to its name, being flowery, highly scented and feminine. It can be chilled, though is better at room temperature.

Chiroubles Strongly cherry-scented and early maturing, Chiroubles should be drunk young.

Morgon Quite tough to start out, this develops amazing kirsch-like aromas and startling intensity.

Regnié The latest village to achieve *Cru* status, Regnié is like a good Beaujolais-Villages. Drink it young.

Brouilly and Côte de Brouilly The Côte de Brouilly is the more distinguished of these; both are luscious, rich and fruity.

The Loire

 I'VE ALWAYS FOOLISHLY imagined that rivers should naturally run from north to south. Looking at a map, it seems impossible that they could manage to climb up from the bottom of the page to the top. But that is exactly the course taken by the River Loire. It has its source deep in the south of France, down in beautiful Ardèche, and ambles north parallel to the Rhône for a time (the Rhône running in the opposite direction, however) before tilting off to the west and continuing to cut across the northern part of the country, east to west, from Orléans to its mouth in Brittany at Nantes.

The vineyards of the Loire valley are mostly concentrated around the river and its tributaries in the northerly east–west stretch, and being in the cooler north, the resultant wines tend to be delicate and light in style, with whites dominating, although there are some sweet treats to be had as well – plus some flavoursome pale reds (unfortunately not seen very widely over here).

The Wines and Their Taste:

Anjou

Anjou in one of its many guises is likely to be one of the first names new wine drinkers come across ... more's the pity. I'll admit there are good wines with this easy-to-pronounce name on the label, but they are in the minority. Most white and rosé Anjous are mean, wretched individuals, victims of over-production and over-sulphuring. If you ever feel a rasping catch in the throat, that's sulphur, used at various stages throughout the wine-making process. It's an essential additive, but should be used with moderation; too much can ruin a wine. The large wine-making area entitled to the name Anjou is up-river from Muscadet. White Anjou relies on the classic white grape variety of the Loire, Chenin Blanc, occasionally beefed up (to its advantage) with a little Chardonnay; reds may depend on Cabernet (either Franc or Sauvignon), Gamay, or the uninspiring local Groslot. Rosés, probably the best known Anjous, may occasionally be made from Cabernet (and will boast this on the label) or more likely from the Groslot.

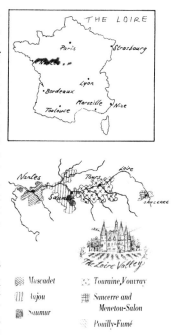

Muscadet   Touraine, Vouvray

Anjou   Sancerre and Menetou-Salon

Saumur

Pouilly-Fumé

White The most obvious scent that wafts off a glass of Chenin from the Loire is unmentionable ... breathe in the bouquet and see if you can see what I mean! It's an odd grape, this Chenin, behaving differently wherever it puts down its roots. In Anjou Blanc there's an association with damp straw, an apparent sickly sweetness on the nose that turns out to be a mirage. The wine is more likely caustically dry, with possibly an overlay of sweetness tagged on; certainly not derived from ripe grapes brimming with sugar.

Red There's a vibrance to the reds of the Loire, almost a vivacity. To look at, they are light and glinting. On the bouquet, there's often a rapier edge to tickle the nostrils, warning the taste buds to expect something a little sharp. And indeed, you'll usually find a sharp zing hiding somewhere in the taste, a slightly metallic tinge, perhaps, but surrounded by cakey softness. Red Anjous can be chilled like white wines and treated in much the same way, either served before food, or partnering light, summery dishes: salads, cold meats, pilafs. Since it's as well to drink them young, the summer is a good time for them – as soon as the new vintage is released.

Rosé The trouble with lots of rosés – Anjou in particular – is sulphur; they're often dosed with too much. Get a good one, though, and you'll find wild strawberries in there – sometimes so concentrated that you could wonder for a moment if the wine were actually fruit flavoured. Your wondering won't last long, though, because the other characteristic aroma of this wine is dirty dish cloths. Few rosé wines are bone dry, and this is no exception. It feels syrupy and soft rather than actively sweet, with all the hard edges mollified. Good examples are the exception, unfortunately. If you find a good one, drink it young and *cold*; don't be afraid of over-chilling it; straight out of the fridge or an ice bucket will do and then use it as a daytime standby; drinks in the garden, before and with lunch or on a picnic, pulled up well chilled from a river.

Cabernet d'Anjou There's a distinct cakiness you'll notice on the bouquet of Cabernet rosés, which dies once you have a sip and is then succeeded by blackcurranty fruit (if you're lucky) and a tinge of sugary sweetness.

Vin de Pays du **Jardin de la France**

The Garden of France: so the Loire Valley is called, every inch of it, and this regional *Vin de Pays* covers the whole area and all its grape varieties. *Vin de Pays* is simple country wine – generally a step up from rock bottom plonk, but simple stuff and cheap. A single tasting note isn't possible for a wine from such a huge, diverse area.

Muscadet

Muscadet's popularity never ceases to surprise me. Not only do individual examples of this often thoroughly lacklustre white not deserve the attention they get, but I can't help thinking that admiration for the whole class of Muscadets is misdirected. It seems to be based on the belief that because Muscadets are very widely available, they must be easy to appreciate; but not so. They are among the driest wines produced, searingly dry and pretty high in acidity. Neither of these features makes them easy to love, so anyone considering Muscadet a 'safe' choice is likely to be in for a surprise – and that's even if they are lucky enough to find a good example; should they find a poor one, they'll be in not for a surprise, but a shock.

Muscadet comes from Pays Nantais, the large area near the mouth of the River Loire. The area surrounding the tributaries of the River Sèvre and the River Maine is credited with producing the best Muscadet (identified on the label as 'de Sèvre et Maine'). An extra mark of quality to look out for is 'sur lie', meaning the wine was kept in contact with the sediment caused by fermentation until it was bottled; this adds woomph and body to the wine and increases the fruitiness. All Muscadets are made from the grape of the same name, the Muscadet (alias Melon de Bourgogne) which is little known elsewhere.

Muscadet is a real sucker for sulphur. Stick your nose in a just-poured glass, and you may well be fought back by the fusty stink of rotting clothes. Possibly because the intrinsic scents and flavours of Muscadet themselves are so slight, the sulphur really shows . . . or perhaps Muscadets are just over-sulphured (I rather think the latter, since even some supposedly 'organic' versions rate pretty highly on the sulphur equivalent of the Richter scale). But there's no getting away from it; it's generally there, clouding the (admittedly faint and anonymous) bouquet. Get past the nose and into the taste and, in a good (generally 'sur lie') version, you can pick up the faint waft of flowers. There's a definite citrusy edge blended with the flavour of unripe melons (this bit I'll freely admit could be auto-suggestion prompted by the synonym for the Muscadet grape, Melon de Bourgogne). An appley freshness is lurking in there, too, like Granny Smiths apples with the skins still on. Interrogate your taste buds more thoroughly, and they may give you the flavour of hay (you'll recognise this only if you've played the country yokel as I have and chewed some between your teeth).

Astringence is common to all Muscadets, the sort that makes your mouth water – almost feeling cleansing like a mouth wash. There is also an unavoidable tartness. In poor versions, these are the two dominant sensations; 'caustic' is what I frequently write in my tasting notes.

Classically, Muscadet is supposed to accompany seafood. It's frequently on sale in wine bars, but for my money I'd rather drink something with a bit more personality on its own, without food. Or I'd friendlify it with a suggestion of crème de cassis (blackcurrant liqueur) in the bottom of the glass or crème de mûre (made from blackberries).

Pouilly-Fumé

Generally a more substantial version of Sancerre, Pouilly-Fumé is richer and more intense, made

from 100 per cent Sauvignon Blanc with the associated green, goosegog flavours. There's a creaminess to it and a definite lemony edge – like a lemon pudding (without the sugar). A handsome white wine to serve with special 'white wine' food such as chicken or fish in a rich creamy sauce. It also goes surprisingly well with herby cheeses.

Sancerre

Sancerre sprang from relative obscurity a quarter of a century ago to being one of the most fashionable white wines in France, and in upwardly mobile circles in Britain – especially when chosen from restaurant wine lists where it features strongly (and often expensively). It is made on the left bank of the Loire where it turns from south-east to south, on the opposite bank from Pouilly-Fumé (one of the most fashionable wines in the US, incidentally). The village of Sancerre itself is perched on a hill rising up from the valley and with thirteen surrounding villages is responsible for producing this steely dry white wine made 100 per cent from Sauvignon Blanc grapes. Menetou-Salon is similar in style – and generally cheaper. Red and a rosé Sancerres made from the Burgundian red grape, the Pinot Noir, are also made in a comparatively minor way.

The Sauvignon is a highly characteristic white grape with a very distinctive smell and flavour. If ever you come across a wine that seems to be green in its bouquet and taste, it is most likely made from the Sauvignon. It recalls newly cut grass, unripe green fruit – principally gooseberries – and, especially in Sancerre, asparagus. The whiff of cats is another Sauvignon give-away, apparent occasionally in Sancerre, but more often in even greener, more astringent Sauvignons made elsewhere in France and in the new world.

Sancerre generally has a little bit more weight; more substance and a smidgen more fruit to it than some rivals; although dead dry and squeaky clean, it does have an assertive personality, unlike, say, the platitudinous Muscadet. And it is a very good food wine, especially good with fish – particularly rich and oily fish such as salmon. It must be admitted that there is quite a chasm of quality difference from the best and the worse, but to give all Sancerres an equal chance of performing at their best, drink them young – within two years of the vintage – and well chilled.

Touraine

The area known as Touraine surrounds the town of Tours towards the eastern edge of the east–west stretch of the river, and harbours some of the Loire's great wines. Best known is Vouvray; deserving equal recognition (although flagging considerably in the availability stakes) are the lovely light, bright Cabernet Franc-based reds of Chinon, Bourgueil and St-Nicolas-de-Bourgueil. But the wine cornering an increasing share of shelf space for itself in Britain is Touraine Sauvignon, which could be described as a poor relation of Sancerre. Touraine Gamay has come on by leaps and bounds as well but as yet Touraine Chardonnay is trailing in the likeability stakes.

Touraine Sauvignon **This is Sauvignon at its steeliest, sometimes with a rapier cutting edge. There is an austerity, an unripeness to this white, leaving the grassy-green characteristics of the Sauvignon stripped bare, accentuating the austere tartness of the unripe gooseberry.**

Touraine Gamay **This red is one of the best Gamays you'll find outside Beaujolais, with bags of cherry fruit on the nose tinged by that characteristic edge of rubber and tar. Direct, piercing fruit on the taste, it can seem sweet and tart at the same time with a suggestion of fruit kernels. Chill it down and glug it down, that's my advice!**

Vouvray

Vouvray means different things to different people. Old school wine buffs conjure up visions of marvellously long-lived honeyed treats offsetting fruity sweetness with an acidity that keeps them fresh for decades. Contemporary wine fans consider Vouvray to be more an affordable unspectacular glass of either dry or medium white wine, still or sparkling, ranging in quality from mediocre to poor. The fact is that Vouvray comes in almost every style (and every quality) imaginable. It can be dry, medium dry, medium sweet, sweet (or *moelleux*) and super-sweet; still, slightly fizzy or sparkling. For a while, the fashion for dry wines kept the sweeties off the shelves, but the classic off-dry Vouvrays are now back in force with their intense honey bouquets and their slight resemblance to wet wool. Chenin Blanc is the base grape for all styles.
Loire Chenins, and particularly the 'medium' Vouvrays, can have a milkiness to them, a sort of

cheesy quality where the milk has turned. This is in part down to the Chenin, but in part, too, to the over-sulphuring that goes on relentlessly along the Loire valley. In the best among them, there is a fruit-salady (with a heavy hand on the kiwi fruit) taste. Although there is an element of sweetness, owing to the naturally very high acidity of the Chenin, this is cut by a fresh zest giving a satisfying balance. These are very good aperitifs and 'first course' wines, going extremely well with pâtés and mousses, corn on the cob, vegetable concoctions, strongly flavoured fish and cheese dishes; demi-sec Vouvrays are good served at the end of a meal, too, being admirable (and unexpected) partners for cheese.

The Rhône

 THE RHÔNE is to red wines what the Loire is to whites. The vineyards around the majestic, deep-cleaving river sourced on the Swiss side of Lake Geneva and running down to the mouth at Marseille, are responsible for all manner of wines including sweet and sparkling, but it is the reds that dominate, ranging from simple glassfuls designed to be tipped down without a thought, to illustrious vintage wines from highly prized sites demanding (with every justification) high prices. Simple Côtes du Rhône is France's best selling wine in Britain; find me a wine shop without an example on sale. And Muscat de Beaumes de Venise, a *vin doux naturel* (which means it is sweet, and on the face of it not particularly *naturel*, being fortified with *eau de vie*), is probably also the best known dessert wine, much loved by restaurants who peddle individual glasses with their sweet trolley.

There are curiosities made along the banks, too, such as the inordinately priced Condrieu made from the Viognier grape, a recherché dry white wine from the north of the wine-producing region recalling the taste of apricots; and the even more exclusive Château Grillet, a rarefied version of the same, coming from a single privately owned seven-acre vineyard, uniquely entitled to its own individual *appellation*.

The vineyards fall into two independent galaxies (although the gap between them is now also beginning to be planted with vines, such is the appetite for Rhônes). The northern (and generally superior) constellation runs from Vienne to Valence, and the generally less brilliant area of the southern Rhône spreads out from Ardèche to Avignon. In the north, the Syrah grape reigns supreme for reds, with Viognier, Marsanne and Rousanne taking care of whites.

In the south, where the bulk of Côtes du Rhône is produced, all sorts of other candidates make their way into the wines. Grenache, in both its red and its white incarnations, is important plus, in the red line, the southern French favourites of Cinsaut and Carignan, as well as more unusual local oddities. Châteauneuf-du-Pape is proud of the thirteen different grape types that can go to make up the blend.

The Wines and Their Taste:

Vin de Pays des Coteaux de l'**Ardèche**

There's a fashionable tendency down in the Ardèche to make wines from single varieties – varieties with which we are happily familiar, such as Syrah, Cabernet Sauvignon, Gamay, Merlot and even Pinot Noir for the reds, and Chardonnay for the whites. There are blends, too, centring on a more general southern Rhône cocktail. Best varietals are good old Cab Sauv, Syrah and Gamay, with Chardonnay coming along a treat as well in an affordably priced way.

Vin de Pays des **Bouches du Rhône**

Country wine from the far south, here and there around the delta of the Rhône, this wine hails from the *département* of the same name.

It's cheap and cheerful stuff, this, can have sweet fruit, may have that 'cakey' flavour of southern French reds and almost certainly will appear a bit dusty. Don't hang around examining it too carefully though, that's certainly not what it is intended for; instead consider it a party wine, good for buffets where it won't offend anything or anyone.

Châteauneuf-du-Pape

Because thirteen different grape varieties – both red and white – can go into this (sometimes) marvellous red wine of the magical name, as you can imagine there is a range of styles and qualities. The best wines are named after an individual property or domaine. And these are well worth the £5, £6 or even £7 asked for them; as I wrote in one tasting note they can have 'the works in there and all working wonderfully together'.

You don't have to put your nose far into the glass to get the bouquet, it comes to meet you with the lovely aroma of the rumtopf; fruit preserved in alcohol. It is a big bouquet, rich in fruit, and you

can almost smell the heat and the sun. There's an edge of ink there, too, and a lovely clean, penetrating slick of fresh paint.

To taste, the promising fruity tones blossom into marvellous sweet fruit . . . held in an iron punnet; there's a hard edge which takes you into some hot peppery flavours with a hint of tobacco. The peppery sensation lingers in the mouth for several moments once you've swallowed. And on the subject of iron, curiously there is a slight hint of iron in the taste, too; that broad almost rusty flavour you get from water drawn from an iron-rich chalybeate health spa spring. Châteauneuf-du-Pape can be a big, hefty wine quite high in alcohol and is therefore not a candidate for sipping on the lawn on a hot summer's day. No, it's more a winter wine, being the measure for casseroles and game.

There is also a white Châteauneuf-du-Pape, less frequently seen, but worth looking out for: a zippy, fresh, highly scented mouthful when drunk young.

Hermitage

Red Hermitage is one of the great aristocrats of the northern Rhône, coming from a single hill, following the contours of the east bank of the river at Tain l'Hermitage. It is made from the Rhône's top red grape, the Syrah (with sometimes the addition of some white Marsanne).

Crozes-Hermitage   The less lustrous surrounding vineyards combine to make Crozes-Hermitage, a humbler relation of Hermitage; not all that humble, though, there are some very good well-priced wines behind this label, worth looking out for on restaurant wine lists. The Syrah is the grape behind the wine.

A wine redolent of goulash flavours; there's a heat to it, meat, spice and a delectable richness. Also on the bouquet, there's the hint of biscuits straight out of the oven with a slight twang of burnt toast. And on the taste you can feel (in a good example, that is) the well-judged orchestration between fruit and tannin. There can be a slight metallic quality, seeming simply to add zing, plus the inevitable spicy pepperiness so typical of the Syrah grape. The old cheesy foot creeps in there, too, but don't be put off, it's an attractive scent when found (in moderation) in a wine, and is an inevitable connotation to many reds of France's south. A 'food' wine, definitely, being a good match

Château Grillet & Condrieu	Coteaux du Tricastin
Condrieu & St Joseph	Beaumes de Venise
St Joseph	Côtes du Ventoux
Crozes-Hermitage & Hermitage	Lirac
Côtes du Rhône & Côtes du Rhône Villages	Tavel
	Châteauneuf-du-Pape
Coteaux de l'Ardèche	Côtes de Lubéron
Côtes de Vivarais	

for dishes with their own woomph such as goulash, steak and kidney or coq au vin.

Côtes du **Lubéron**

At the southern end of the southern Rhône, this little enclave has recently been promoted from VDQS status to full *Appellation Contrôlée*. It produces light, but strongly flavoured reds (with some stars among them, notably the Val-Joanis wines).

The pepperiness on some examples is strong enough to help you imagine you are sniffing a pepper pot. You are led to believe that when you take a sip you'll be in for something pretty hefty; strong flavours are hinted at. But it's surprising how light on actual flavour, substantial fruity flavour, that is, these wines can be. There's pepper on the palate, enough to give the tongue a start, but not much more in the way of individual character. But they are cheerful enough and good to splash down with simple grub along the shepherd's pie or cauliflower cheese lines.

Côtes du **Rhône**

What a melting pot of styles and qualities! I suppose the best advice I can give in finding a good one is to look for one named after a single property, a domaine; but Côtes du Rhône isn't exactly trying to give itself airs and graces, it's just made to be drunk. *'Vin du Soleil'* is how it is advertised by the roadside of the Autoroute to the south, 'wine of the sun', and there's certainly no shortage of the latter. Before modern technology came up with ways of dealing with protracted blasts of hot summer sun, it used to be too much of a good thing, breeding beefy wines top heavy with alcohol; now lighter styles prevail (frequently disciples of the *macération carbonique* method, see page 26). Wines with the handle *Villages* added to their name come from the best sites and are generally superior and longer lived. The best of the Côtes du Rhône Villages wines now have their own *appellations*, Gigondas and Vacqueyras.

Red Côtes du Rhône is generally now more like Beaujolais, but earthier and without the pzazz and the bite . . . or, regrettably, it can be like sucking an old leather boot, or be quite unremarkable in every respect. It varies a lot, as you can see, and sadly I cannot safeguard you against getting a bad one. But let's not dwell on that. What is it like at its best? Because of the cocktail of grapes, there's inevitably going to be a slightly leathery smell (in Australia, they attribute the Shiraz grape – the Rhône's Syrah – with the scent of a 'sweaty saddle'; imagine the saddle, in this instance, without the sweat), so it can be mellow and comforting. Investigate further, and the leathery notes may acquire the slight tinge of the cheesy foot but, before you hose the rest of the glass down the sink without a second chance, look further, there is some attractive cherry fruit in there, perhaps a suggestion of sharp damson tart and a hint of spice. The Grenache may contribute a dusty edge to pepper the grapey confectionery-counter sweetness. All versions should be drunk young, at least within three years, and the juicy-fruity light style types can be chilled, when they become highly versatile glugging wines; okay served on their own, equally at home with casual food; they're not up to the full-blown dinner party, but go well with the shepherd's pie, nut cutlet, chilli con carne, spaghetti bolognese sort of meal.

White White Côtes du Rhône is produced in much smaller volume (3 million bottles per year to the red equivalent's 200 million) and is generally fresh and gluggable if caught in its infancy.

Tavel Rosé

France's best loved rosé . . . in France; regrettably we don't see Tavel as often in Britain as we should, because it's really *delicious*. It can be made from the same grapes as Côtes du Rhône, but in practice generally centres on Grenache. Tavel is always dry and quite alcoholic for a rosé. The old style used to be rusty coloured, wood-aged wines, but it is more common now to make raspberry pink, fresh-as-a-daisy types.

Far removed from the usual run-of-the-mill rosés, this one has cut and thrust and style. Dip your nose into the glass and you'll immediately be aware of a challenging dry edge softened by hints of wild strawberries. Into the taste, and there's not a single off flavour in sight; just alluring uncluttered fruit, still dwelling on the strawberry theme, crisp and clean and finishing neatly with a faint prickle of acidity. More expensive than bog standard rosés, I'll grant you, but it's worth it. Marvellous for summer meals, Tavel is up to anything you'd care to put with it – even red meat – although it's delicate enough for seafood and fish as well; a great partner for salmon.

Coteaux du **Tricastin**

This pocket of the southern Rhône just south of Montelimar, produces red wines with unusual talent. The southern Rhône grape medley (Grenache, Cinsaut, Syrah, Mourvèdre and Carignan) here combines to make fragrant, fruity wines with a whiff of ink on the nose leading you on into flower scented tastes and rich, ripe, come-and-get-me flavours.

Côtes du **Ventoux**

A light southern Rhône red with the scents of warm simmering jam, piercing fruit cuts through the hot-country wine flab giving a welcome freshness. It has a slightly hollow taste, without enough stuffing in the middle, a bit feeble, but good if you're in the mood for something light and zingy to wash down a lasagne or spaghetti bolognese.

The South-East

The Wines and Their Taste:

Coteaux d'**Aix-en-Provence**

Taking care of western Provence inland from Marseille, this large *appellation* has some excellent estates working miracles, particularly with reds. There is commitment to planting better grapes – notably Cabernet Sauvignon and Syrah – to produce some stunning 'Provence clarets'.

There's a herby, minty twist to the bouquet of these lovely bright, piercing reds, reminiscent of water meadow plants; and a refreshing directness to the raspberry fruitiness delicately balanced by a refreshing acidity. The fruit gives way to a drying edge on the tongue – like the effect of eating plum skins – and leaves a tart cleansing feel to the mouth.

Lovely and refreshing chilled; this is an up-cheering red wine, light and spritely and vigorous. Good for summer evenings, you can drink it without food or with uncomplicated dishes such as cold spreads, pizza and pasta.

Corbières

One of the biggest wine names in the south of France, Corbières comes from the south-east, between Narbonne and Perpignan. A prolific wine-producing area formerly wallowing in massive yields, it now competes in the market place more on the grounds of quality (Corbières was elevated to the dignified *Appellation Contrôlée* status in 1985). Rouge is the thing down here, although minimal quantities of white and rosé are produced also. Four triggers for the white are lemon, sherbet, custard and a hint of peardrops. The typical Mediterranean grape varieties of Carignan, Grenache, Cinsaut and a bit of Syrah dominate the blend for reds (where they may be joined by other local 'also-rans'), and the wines may be vinified either traditionally (producing big, meaty types) or in the classic Beaujolais method, known as *macération carbonique*, whereby the grapes are fermented whole to increase fruitiness and cut down on tannin.

Vinified traditionally, these wines cannot escape the thud of tough meatiness characteristic of the wines of the Midi. The robust local vine varieties bake under the hot sun and bear fruit . . . tinged by the unmistakable aroma of feet. (Don't be alarmed, no feet are involved in the vinification process; there's just a suggestion of their aroma in many classic Mediterranean wines.) And there's nothing much wrong with that, so long as you're in the mood for it, and the rest of the flavour orchestration is appealing in its way. Young versions are spritely papal purple in colour and there is a pepperiness, a spiciness to the bouquet with a slight sense of that characteristic dustiness associated with the Grenache, discernible both on the nose and, curiously, in the taste. Okay, so maybe something liquid can't actually *be* dusty, but it can taste as though it is. Look also for a faint tinge of liquorice before you swallow, when you'll feel a dryness in the mouth (which comes from the tannin – the same ingredient that makes tea leaves seem parching, too). Definitely a 'with food' wine – preferably meaty or root vegetably, and substantial.

Coteaux du Languedoc

Minervois

Corbières

Fitou

Côtes du Roussillon

Vin de Pays du Gard

Coteaux d'Aix-en-Provence

Côtes de Provence

Vin de Corse

Vin de Pays de l'Hérault

The
Key to
Wine-tasting

The secret of how to taste wine to get the most out of it:
Holding the glass by the stem, first look at the wine against
a white background. It should be clear and the colour will
hint at its age and character (see page 13).

Now for the swirling. By disrupting the surface of the wine, you release maximum bouquet into the bowl of the glass. Do this by gently swirling the glass either in the air or, if you feel safer, on a table. Perhaps practise with water first.

The bouquet of a wine can tell you as much as the taste. To get the most out of it you must sniff really deeply with your nose right in the glass. Because your sense of smell is short-lived, take a break between sniffs.

When you drink wine socially, there's not much of an art to sipping. If you want to discover more about the wine though, there's a whole rigmarole you can follow. First take a sip, then chew it around your mouth so it coats all surfaces.
Don't swallow yet!

Keeping that first sip in your mouth, purse your lips as though you're about to whistle and draw air in through your mouth so it passes over the wine on your tongue and carries the bouquet to the back of your throat where your nose picks it up.

At last you can swallow! By going through this routine, you should discover all sorts of scents and flavours from that single sip which would have eluded you if you'd just sipped and swallowed in the normal way. Now enjoy the rest of the glass in peace.

Vin de **Corse**

Although French, Corsica nestles under Italy's armpit and includes characteristics of the wines of both countries in her own produce. She has her own peculiar Italian-inspired grape varieties, to which are added for reds, the old favourites among southern French grapes, Carignan, Cinsaut, Grenache *et al*; while the spritzy, lemony Vermentino grape (also widely used in Sardinia) sews up the whites.

There's a slight smell of old boots to some of the reds, tinged with beeswax. Although traditionally, Corsican wines have been quite big and beefy, they are moving with the times towards a lighter, juicier style. Tasting a little like a fermenting fruit salad (heavy on slightly unripe plums) there is a vibrance to these wines, sparked by the sort of lively acidity you expect from the Italians.

Fitou

A sudden fashion for this inky dark wine in its distinctive dark, high shouldered bottles with their extra long labels swept Britain quite unaccountably in the eighties, and caught up in the enthusiasm all sorts of unlikely customers who'd previously been 'white-wine-only' fans. And there could have been few less appropriate wines to persuade them on to reds, for it is a mighty beast in even its most friendly guise. (But such is the way with fashions generally – quite unaccountable.) Not that there's anything wrong with Fitou, far from it; it is one of the first wines from the far south of France to achieve *Appellation Contrôlée* status, in vineyards near the sea in the *département* of the Aude. But being made largely from the southern Carignan grape, it can be rough, tough and powerful.

The scents and flavours of Fitou put me in mind of an old leather chair. Leathery notes, with perhaps a suggestion of creamy saddle soap. There's a hard backbone in there mollified by modest helpings of sweet fruit. It's not all sweet, though, oh no; be prepared for the drying edge of sloes or tart damsons with tough, thick skins. There's an inkiness to this wine, too – and that's not merely auto-suggestion from the colour; it actually reminds me of the taste of ink – or the smell of ink, if you like. I can't imagine everyone can recall the taste of their ink wells; I certainly can, even as a child I was obsessed with taste and smell.

Vin de Pays du **Gard/Costières de Nîmes**

I have linked these two together, because up until the harvest of 1989, Costières de Nîmes was called Costières du Gard – the name switch being initiated by the better quality Costières producers who wanted to set themselves apart from what they considered to be the riff-raff. The large, arid stretch between Nîmes and Montpellier is entitled to the Costières *appellation* for its cheap and cheerful reds from a cocktail of meaty southern grapes (Carignan, Cinsaut, Mourvèdre, Grenache and Syrah), plus a little white and rosé. The humbler Vin de Pays handle is available to wines throughout the whole *département* of Gard, including lesser beings from the same cocktail and, interesting this, wines made from untypical grapes for the area such as the noble Merlot and Cabernet Sauvignon. These are the stars, packing in lovely juicy, accessible fruit into the glass rather than the customary meaty, tarry flavours of the region's own grapes.

Vin de Pays de l'**Hérault**

Grape varieties have their natural habitats; areas where, for centuries they have put down their roots and have been blessed by the law so to do. When wine-making was much more insular and you simply continued to plant what your father had before and follow his tried and tested methods, there was neither an exchange of ideas nor an exchange of grapes and methods. Now both travel enthusiastically, and the l'Hérault is where many 'outside' grapes from other regions end up; it is a hotbed of experimentation. So if I tell you a Vin de Pays de l'Hérault tastes like this, you'll have one of the increasing numbers of 'exceptions to the rule' in your glass to tell me it tastes instead . . . like that. Outsider varieties that are doing particularly well are Merlot and Cabernet Sauvignon, producing marvellously velvety claretesque treats. Trad wines for the area, though, are largely red and rely on the Cinsaut and Carignan with Grenache and a little Mourvèdre and Syrah. There are many smaller Vins de Pays made on more or less the same lines such as Vin de Pays d'Aude, Vallée de Paradis and Collines de la Mourne.

The bouquet seems dry and drying to the inquisitive nostrils, offering a twitch of pepperiness. On the taste you can find in varying proportions, farmyard tendencies and rich plummy fruit. The hot, spicy pepper from the bouquet fulfils its threat

and continues into the taste where it actually marries in well with the other components.

Coteaux du **Languedoc**

This is the collective term for a string of wine-producing villages mainly in the Hérault *département*, the best of which attach their village name to the general *appellation*. The law's precise rules as to the grapes and their proportions are shifting a bit to encourage greater emphasis on the more interesting varieties. The whole of France's deep south, in fact, is a shifting sand of grape varieties, concentrating more and more on the more rewarding types.

There's a distinct puttiness to the reds, glinting through the hot cakey aura. The fruit and the cakiness become blended on the palate to give the impression of rich, alcoholic fruit cake; Guinness cake, in fact. St Chinian is an individual *Cru* village wine to look out for, with its green-tinged fruit and earthy, stony associations in the taste.

Minervois

Made in the thick of Languedoc-Roussillon, France's largest wine area hugging the Mediterranean coast, the twist to the usual grape medley for Minervois (virtually all red, incidentally) is a high proportion of Carignan grapes. These wines only earned their *Appellation Contrôlée* status in 1985, and some examples, you might think, still don't really deserve it, but there are excellent exceptions.

The bouquet collecting in a glass of a good Minervois could remind you of sticking your nose into a box containing a mixture of chocolates and crystallised fruits, with the grapey, yeasty scents of a winery in full swing as a backdrop. But your heady reverie will be broken soon enough when you take a sip, although the raspberry fruitiness continues, it is slightly drowned out by the tough southern thud you expect from the reds of the Midi. If well made and kept on its toes, though, Minervois can be light, fresh and have attractive astringence at the end of the mouthful. Food partners? It has to be roasts and stews; an ideal companion for good home cooking.

Côtes de **Provence**

The marvellously holiday-minded, pine-scented, wild herb-strewn hills and dales sweeping down to the Mediter-

ranean around St Tropez in the *département* of Var make
wines with holidays in mind. Rosés dominate in exotic
shaped bottles, followed by fruity, come-and-get-me reds
and a handful of increasingly zippy whites. This is a catch-
all name for all comers from the area. Although it is a full-
blown *Appellation Contrôlée*, it appears to be a more
forgiving one than most letting all manner of wines limbo
in (some being more deserving than others). Bandol is a
little catchment within the area producing some of the
best wines, the reds being spicy and solid, needing several
years to mature; the whites being fresh and fragrant; and
the rosés being a softer mirror of the excellent reds.

Rosé   Things are improving, but by golly they
needed to! The quality of rosé world-wide has
flagged behind the other two colours and here,
since there was a sitting market ready and waiting
on the beaches of the Riviera, there seemed to be
even more of an excuse not to try. So although the
coral-coloured liquid gushing out of the variously
shaped bottles is now at least clean, it still errs on
the side of the uninteresting. There's invariably a
sweet cakey edge to the bouquet, like doughy scones
before they are fully cooked. On the palate you *may*
find a hint of wild strawberry fruit, but like as not it
will be sandwiched between hints of nail polish
remover and pine (as in a disinfectant bottle). Not a
wine to keep, this should be drunk as young as possible. It must be icy cold when served, and goes
curiously well with spicier dishes than you might
imagine; try it with cold meats and sausages, pâté,
garlicky soups and sauces.

Red   Although Côtes de Provence has the ability
to cover a multitude of sins, being a whopping great
catchment area in the hot south, the reds hold their
heads up well in any (comparably priced) company. There are some eager wine-makers down in
this holiday strip, experimenting away like crazy
with the long list of grapes legally at their disposal.
Cabernet Sauvignon is legitimate here (up to 30
per cent of the blend) and purply fruit is the aim,
with its piercing, direct pungence cut with lively
and surprising acidity. There's an inky, meaty
quality to some of these reds, reminiscent of good
flavoursome gravy. They can be a bit hard, but generally there is enough fruit to balance. But it is possible to find quite a range of individual styles
encompassed within this one *appellation*. The

more streamlined, friendly/fruity styles can be chilled and are good out of doors at summer parties and picnics.

White Not the area's most promising style (and far from its greatest output), these rather ordinary dry whites can at best be soft and flowery, but tend to tire quickly and are coarse and lumbering unless tackled in their early youth.

Côtes du **Roussillon**

The couple of thousand years experience in making wine in Roussillon around Perpignan didn't appear to have been to much avail until the last decade. This has been committed wine lake country, with the apparent motto 'never mind the quality, feel the volume', but mercifully, at last, incentives to do better have paid off, and there has been an astonishing improvement in quality with a visible striving for excellence. The grape medley for reds concentrates on the tough, sturdy Carignan, with a handful of more amusing types, while an increase in Macabeo has done wonders to spice up the better whites.

Although pale and translucent, red Côtes du Rousillon is a hot wine, make no mistake. There's a warm cakiness that lifts off the bouquet and a warm, sunny feel to the taste. A good fruity wallop conjuring up the scent and flavour of prunes, is tweaked by a sprinkling of spice and a hint of tar. Good glugging plonk, warm and comforting on a cool evening and well matched to casseroles and the like and vegetarian alternatives.

The South-West

The Wines and Their Taste:

Bergerac

Inland from Bordeaux, upstream along the Dordogne river, Bergerac is a rippling reflection of the world's greatest wine-producing area. I say rippling because it never in its wildest fantasies lives up to the glossy glory of great Bordeaux; it is also inconsistent in quality. But good Bergerac is certainly a match for many an ordinary Bordeaux, red or white, and its rosés are vivid and attractive. The grapes upon which these wines rely are the same as for Bordeaux, with Cabernet Sauvignon, Cabernet Franc, Merlot and Malbec heading up the reds, and Sémillon, Sauvignon and Muscadelle being responsible for the whites. A good name to look out for is Château la Jaubertie, where the highly individual wines are made by an Englishman. You'll find the same mix of grapes and styles also coming from nearby Côtes de Duras, very much an up and coming area.

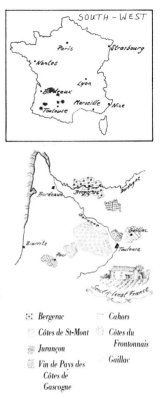

:: Bergerac
Côtes de St-Mont
Jurançon
Vin de Pays des Côtes de Gascogne

Cahors
Côtes du Frontonnais
Gaillac

Red At best, these wines can pack all the blackberry fruit you want into the glass, cut by a delicious minty edge. Early maturing, they tend to give all they've got in their youth, and so with rare exceptions (typically those that have been aged in oak barrels, this will be expressed on front or back label, most probably) should be drunk young; four years old maximum. Good zingy fruit is the thing, if it is lacking they can be rather tough and tannic, giving a furry feel to the tongue.

Sec Historically, white Bergerac was all sweet, but with increased plantings of the Sauvignon grape, they have gradually edged towards the dry (going through the doldrums also suffered by white Bordeaux a decade or so back, when they were unforgivably soupy – a little bit 'sicky' if one is to be honest) on the way to their clipped, fresh new style. Brave new Bergerac Sec, as the dry white is called, is just that, and when well made combines the rapier dry Sauvignon with the softer Sémillon to produce a round, ripe, slightly appley white wine. Some Sauvignon-only wines are produced and these can be too aggressively tart and unripe-gooseberryish.

Rosé Usually intensely pretty in the blue-pink genre with penetrating fruitgum flavours.

Cahors

Traditionally known as black wine, Cahors now no longer really lives up to the description. Malbec (the grape from which maximum colour used to be extracted by heavy-handed old-fashioned methods) still accounts for 70 per cent of the recipe though, with Merlot and Tannat largely making up the difference. Cahors' vineyards south-east of Bergerac date back to Roman times, and earned for the wine quite a reputation over the centuries. The reputation has slipped a bit, but now that the wine has at last found its way into twentieth-century favour, it's an interesting invididual in the thunderbolt class.

This powerfully-scented red wine combines on the bouquet hints of wax furniture polish coupled with fleeting associations of an oily rag – and an enticing combination it is as well! The lighter new style Cahors now balance out the raw, rusty first impression and the rather tart aggressive finish with lovely dense pomegranate fruit flavours. It is sumptuous wine in a straitjacket – and purposely so, since the area it comes from majors on rich flavour-packed dishes such as cassoulet and magret de canard. Put it with charcuterie, offal or rich meaty stews and you'll see it's perfectly designed for the job.

Côtes du **Frontonnais/Fronton**

This is an idiosyncratic little red wine from a small area north of Toulouse which, although obscure, is bagging an increasing area of shelf space for itself. And deservedly so. It is made largely from the entirely local Negrette grape, topped up with a variety of old friends from Bordeaux, the southern Rhône and even Beaujolais. But it is the Negrette that by law dominates the potion.

It's not so much the taste as the *feel* of Fronton wines that makes them so individual. A chamois leather smoothness is the thing, the wine being soft as velvet and easy as cream in the mouth (if the wine comes from the cellars of a good wine-maker, that is; nature can't achieve these miracles on her own. Bellevue-la-Forêt is a name worth looking out for). Juicy fruit is another characteristic come-on of this wine, giving it as easy an appeal as you expect from any easy drinking white. Look (or more accurately sniff) more closely and you'll find flower-petal tones and the air of damp rhododendrons or of marshy plants and wild mint. And you may also detect a smattering of nutmeg. There's a spike of acidity in there, too (happily), digging the grape in the ribs and preventing it from becoming too cosy and comfortable for its own good. Perhaps in one's imagination it's possible to have a soft, gentle wine with no contrast, no astringent acidity, but in

reality there's got to be a firm backbone lurking in the middle to cut through the soothing fruitiness of it all; we are talking of wine here and not mere juice.

Gaillac

Ancient wines, now with their own *appellation*, these come from within the larger (generally inferior) Côtes du Tarn catchment. Seen abroad as often in a wine box as a bottle, in its native habitat near Toulouse, Gaillac comes in every colour and guise imaginable, although in Britain the medium dry white incarnation is most frequently seen. Both the red and white rely on lesser known grapes from the area, Duras being the most important player in the reds and Mauzac the whites.

Red Aromatic and essentially light in style with a vibrant – almost fizzy – fruitiness to them, like fizzing boiled sweets. Usually made in the fruit-concentrating *macération carbonique* method (see page 26), they are much lighter on their feet than you might expect. Sometimes the bouquet misfires a bit and gives a slightly nauseous quality. Not as bad as it sounds, and you forget about it if the fruit is forward enough.

White Fresh clean and pure tasting for cheaper 'medium' wines, there's a hint of sponge cake on the nose, leading you into the pretty fruity-with-a-sprinkling-of-sweetness taste. A bit like apple pie, combining a well-balanced mixture of zingy apple fruit (like crunching into a crisp Worcester), soft sweetness and refreshing acidity. There's a fresh citrus edge in there, too. Chilled right down, this is a marvellous summer drinking wine, having plenty to say for itself if served on its own, and being soft and pretty enough to complement chicken or fish, perhaps cooked in a creamy sauce.

Vins de Pays des Côtes de **Gascogne**

Having lead a quiet and unexceptional life in beautiful, bucolic Gascony, the white *Vin de Pays* of the region made a big entrance into the British wine market four years ago and won for itself quite a fan club. It is made in Armagnac country (home of d'Artagnan of Three Musketeers fame) from the same grapes used to make the base wine for distilling into brandy – namely Ugni Blanc and Colombard

– increasingly enlivened by newcomers to enhance the fresh approach. The proportions of the grapes vary from year to year, which has quite an effect on the taste. A little red of the same name is coming to Britain now, looks as pretty as a cherry, but is actually a bit tough and meaty with sometimes an unattractive association with dog food.

Refreshing and dry, there is an aggressive acidity here that adds to the freshness and has a cleansing effect on the mouth. The suggestion of citrus fruits given by the acidity can be offset by the scent and flavour of water melons and exotic fruits (some, it must be said, in fruitgum guise). Less fruity versions offer grassy, twiggy notes and nuances instead. In the best versions (and they do vary, even though there are few sources sending their wines to Britain) there is a good balance between fruit and acidity in a wine of some depth and body. The wines of '88 conjured up the curious scent of shellfish, allegedly a feature of the Colombard grape that year. Although there are plenty of 'triggers' to look for in these attractive dry white wines, it must be said they're not really for pondering over. A quick sniff and swirl and it's time to get on with glugging them down, well chilled, either without food or to accompany fish and seafood (especially the faintly fishy versions).

Jurançon

Wine simply called Jurançon on the label is sweet – well sweetish, anyway; a historic old white wine from Gascony, home of the Three Musketeers. It is made from the local grape varieties Grand and Petit Manseng plus Courbu (if that makes you any the wiser). The dry version has to call itself Jurançon Sec. Neither wine was much seen around until recently when Marks & Spencer spearheaded a revival in Britain with their delicious demi-sec version.

Peaches and cream, that's what both the dry and sweet versions call to mind in their own way (the sweeter ones seem to be sprinkled with more sugar). Even on the dry version, there are sweet clover scents on the bouquet, but when you get into the taste, you stumble into quite a sharp core to the wine, wrapped up in fruit pastels. There's an unusual waxy taste, too, and the lingering fruit of unripe peaches. It makes an unusual change from the old 'dry white' favourites, doubling as a good aperitif wine and a good rapier to cut through plain

food. The sweeter versions are more unusual still – and unusually good. They involve honey in the peachiness and a touch of cinnamon and crystallised fruit. Served in the French way – that is before food or with pâté or salty starters – they are surprisingly delicious. If you want to team them with pudding, make sure it's not too sweet; fruit and fruit tarts are good partners, chocolate éclairs are not.

Côtes de **St-Mont**

This little-known VDQS from way down in swashbuckling Armagnac country has started to make ripples on the wine shop shelves. The red includes the highly fashionable Cabernets (Sauvignon and Franc) plus Merlot along with the local (rather tannic) Tannat, while the white is made from a local medley plus Sauvignon.

Red Here you have a beefy, stewy bouquet cut with sharp rumtopf scents (you know, fruits steeped in alcohol) leading you into a slightly cakey flavour iced with attractive suggestions of blackberries. But there is toughness caught up in this wine, too, a slight astringence and the tart flavours you get from the skins of unripe plums. The toughness comes from tannin and enables the wine to have a long future (if you care to lay it down). I wouldn't bother, but would dish it up right away with game, duck or goose or any other meaty or fatty dish with substance and plenty to say for itself. And for goodness' sake don't even consider teaming it with fish or you'd have a culinary murder on your hands.

White Conjure up the scents of gorse baking on a parched heath and you have the gently honeyed scent and taste of this unusual wine. It reminds me of flowers you don't expect to have a scent – such as gorse and broom; fleetingly sweet, but twiggy and faintly earthy as well.

Italy

ITALY IS THE LARGEST producer of wine in the world, hair-raisingly making about a quarter of its entire production – that is her tragedy. Her own per capita consumption is on the slippery slope downwards each year – that is ours. You see the trouble is that whereas there used to be a hearty appetite at home for Italy's thoroughly Italian wines, once this started to fall away, she had to concentrate hard on finding markets elsewhere. And fearing to enter combat on sheer quality terms with French wines, she made the unfortunate mistake of using price as her weapon, determined to undersell all comers from everywhere.

Her wine laws basically benefit producers aiming to concentrate more on quantity than quality. The permitted yields of grapes per hectare are far higher than those for equivalent French wines – and greater yields lead to reduced concentration of flavour and therefore a slump in essential quality. And it's such a shame! There's something marvellously different and delicious about the Italianness of Italian wines, and for this to be diluted at all is our loss.

But looking on the bright side, as you skim through some of the taste pictures that follow, you'll see that a thoroughly optimistic note creeps in persistently. There are signs of improvement and masses of previously dull, dismal wines are now giving us something to think about. Now quantity isn't seen as the only way ahead. It's one way, certainly, but not the only one.

In the late 1970s a new top-quality classification was introduced for allegedly the 'top wines', trying to steer them, at least, on the lower quantity/higher quality course, where the previous classification had failed. In common with most other countries, Italy's basic quality status for her wines is table wine, called simply *Vino da Tavola*. Next up the scale, you come to *Denominazione di Origine Controllata*, supposedly the same as France's *Appellation Contrôlée*, but in practice less strict. And the new top category is called *Denominazione di Origine Controllata e Garantita*, the *e Garantita* meaning 'and guaranteed', perhaps implying that the ordinary DOC couldn't entirely be relied upon on its own.

Classico is a key word to look for on the label, too. A Classico wine comes from the heart of the region, from the best vineyards generally on a propitiously angled slope. Where expansion of the vineyards has taken place, as in Valpolicella, the overspill is into the unspectacular plains which make only ordinary wines. Although neither slope nor the Classico handle is an absolute guarantee of greater things, in almost all cases (I'll tell you about the exceptions to the rule) it gives the wine a helping hand.

Italy has been at this wine-making – and drinking – lark for longer than most; the vine was first introduced to her country getting on for 3000 years ago, and wine has been made from it ever since. And no country in the world makes such an instantly recognisable style of wine, especially red wine. Get your nose in a glass of *any* Italian red and the first thing it boasts is its nationality. There is an unmistakable Italianness to it, a vibrance, a nervy acidity that you couldn't mistake. For an essentially hot country, her whites are generally very streamlined, especially those from the north, which again have the slightest dance of fizz on the tongue.

Even though the famous names in Italian wines are well known, their natural habitats are not necessarily familiar. There are also many other obscure wines now quite widely available on the shelves so for simplification her wines are simply listed here alphabetically, in case you weren't sure under which region to look for any given wine!

The Wines and Their Taste:

Barbaresco

Coming from east of the town of Alba in Piedmont, Barbaresco is a very close relation of the more famous Barolo, made from the same hefty Nebbiolo grape, and is similar (although less so) in style. Smaller quantities are made than of the noble Barolo, but standards are consistently good – particularly from the Produttori Associati co-op and from Fontanafredda. Beware not to commit infanticide with these red wines (your mouth will pay the price); they need a good five years to mature from the vintage, although the best examples will continue to shine for much longer than that.

Fans of the exorbitantly priced white truffle coming from the same area, say that's what Barbaresco reminds them of, but it's a comparison few of us can afford to make. Humbler taste parallels centre around prunes, with fleeting reminders of raspberries and violets, even a hint of liquorice and chocolate. There's an intensity of flavour to these wines, which before you indulge in it too long is lashed by a characteristically lively acidity. There's tannin galore in there as well (that mouth-drying property you find in grape skins), and the two together can seem in danger of swamping the gentle fruit, but generally it manages to hold its own, despite a tough battle. Many a Barbaresco

will do you proud teamed with a winter stew, a roast
or a steak.

Barbera

Barbera is the red grape variety giving its name to wines
from here and there called Barbera di This and Barbera di
That. The best are from Piedmont, south-east of Turin.

**The most striking attribute of this grape is its
high acidity, positively vibrant, but unless you are
unlucky enough to get a wishy-washy type, there is
generally enough juicy fruity flavour to balance it
out. The fruit content has sweetness and bitterness
all bound up together – like plums with tart skins.
There's also a hint of redcurrants and an intriguing
smokiness. Barbera d'Alba is top of the class, producing the most intense flavours (sometimes
pepped up with oak from barrel maturation, contributing a silky vanilla coating). It can be tackled
very young, though two to three years is more the
norm. Barbera d'Asti is generally lighter in style
and usually drunk in its infancy when it is lovely
glugging stuff. If oak-aged, then this, too, becomes
broader and more voluptuous, although still
retaining the rapier edge. Lightest of all is Barbera
del Monferrato.**

Bardolino

Next-door neighbour of Valpolicella, Bardolino once
shared the same fame, but during a blip in Bardolino's fortunes, Valpolicella got ahead and poor old Bardolino has
been trailing ever since. But it's probably all to
Bardolino's good in the end, over-popularity never did any
wine any good. Anyway, this unloved red wine comes from
the marvellously cheering shores of Lake Garda, where it
is made from the three grapes also responsible for its
neighbour: Corvina, Rondinella and Molinara. Generally
wine from the heart of any wine producing area (identified
as Classico on the label) is the best quality. Here the
Classico wine isn't so much the best as the exception.
Bardolino is a bright and breezy wine – at its best, at its
brightest and breeziest. Classico wines, however, tend to
be fuller and weightier and longer lived, which seems to
miss the point.

**Ripe cherries should gush out of the glass here,
tempered by the more serious edge of bitter almonds. Some wine-makers try to make what they
consider to be more 'serious' wines . . . and gener-**

ally fail dismally in the attempt, coming up with dull, tired leathery old things that do no-one any favours. *Superiore* on the label indicates more alcohol in the bottle; generally an unnecessary – even unwelcome – frill. Fruit and a lovely zippy freshness is the thing here, shown off to advantage if the wine is chilled. A good wine to serve as an aperitif, or to partner spicy cold meats or piquant salads, or if you want a good contrast, to cut through the heaviness of a huge plate of spaghetti.

Bardolino Chiaretto The rosé version of Bardolino (*chiaro* means light) is pretty violetty pink in colour and subtly combines the appley crispness of a white wine with the rounded cherry and strawberry fruit flavours that could come only from a red.

Barolo

Traditionally acknowledged as one of Italy's all-time greats (although there are plenty of British wine lovers who do not – absolutely not – hold that opinion), Barolo, from the sharply pointed hills of Piedmont, south of Turin, is something of an awkward customer. The grape behind this much contested wine is the pesky Nebbiolo, which has its own style of doing things. Unlike other red wine-making grapes, the Nebbiolo's intention is *not* to make life easy for the drinker. Putting out wines that are rich, round and fruity is simply not in its style. Instead they tend to be mighty and tough, taking at least five years to soften enough to be approachable – sometimes much longer (the minimum required by law is three years).

Although fruit is far from being the most obvious feature of this wine, it *is* there, tucked away in the middle of the astringence and the tough, mouth-drying tannins. Close your eyes and concentrate and you can seek out semblances of raspberries and summer-pudding fruits. There's a fleeting hint of violets on the bouquet, and an earthy, meaty, deep, dark mushroomy taste. As a rough guide, the more expensive the Barolo, the more of a challenge it offers to the drinker. Cheaper types are less austere and give the mouth a softer ride. But one thing is for sure, this is no wine to sip out on the terrace on a hot summer's day. It cries out for rich or solid grub as an accompaniment. A hot steamy casserole pepped up with spicy sausage could be just the thing, or game such as venison or hare.

Bianco di Custoza

This is a sort of super-Soave from the Lake Garda area, being based on the same white grape varieties, Garganega and Trebbiano. But there's the difference. I said only *based on*. For poor old Soave that's the whole picture, and to be frank, these aren't the most characterful of grapes, but for Bianco di Custoza there's an option on various others, too, namely Tocai, Cortese, Malvasia and Riesling Italico, which contribute fragrance and fruit in abundance.

Okay, so here at first sip you have a gentle creamy, marginally nutty white wine, but tune up your nosing and tasting antennae and you can pick up the crispness and bite of a cold Granny Smith, the oiliness of just-blanched almonds, the sweet nuttiness of hazels, the mouth-tingling attack of fresh greengages and the richness of a ripe peach. Top that with the elusive scent of hedgerows in spring and you have the complete picture. But all these delightful diversions are subtly integrated into the delicate, restrained taste that, at first, seems to be simply gentle and creamy and very slightly nutty . . . and if you don't feel like it, you need register no more than that. Cool it down and enjoy it for the lovely, fresh, young (it must be young) wine that it is and sip it without food or team it with something light and delicate such as savoury crêpes, risotto or fish pie.

Brunello di Montalcino

A new (in wine terms) star, having been around for a mere hundred years, it comes from Tuscany (where Montalcino is a small village) and is made from the red Brunello grape, whch is actually merely a variation on the Sangiovese/ Chianti grape theme. It is never cheap, but always cheerful in an arm-and-a-leg 'special occasion' sort of way.

A mighty glassful, this, singing with the plum/ prune/tea medley you associate with Chianti, its next of kin. Here on the bouquet you find spice, with cinnamon scents dominating, and in grand old examples, the enveloping aroma of fresh, ripe figs. It has the stewed-tea tannin you'll come to expect from this sort of rich but tough heavyweight, making it a good partner for a surprising variety of foods ranging from the rich through the spicy to the good plain British roast.

Chardonnay

One of the world's most experienced travellers, the Chardonnay has put down roots in Italy too. It is longest established in the north-east corner where it makes a very different style of white wine.

The Chardonnays of Alto Adige (called also Sudtirol) are much slimmer and lighter than you might expect, with a zing of lemon zest and a faint prickle of fizz on the tongue. Look harder, and on top of the characteristic cream-like taste, you'll perhaps find a little nutmeg and the merest suggestion of salt. The Chardonnays of Friuli are a touch richer, better rounded, softer and more floral.

Chianti

Probably the most famous of all Italian wines, although in the past often undeservingly so, gut-rot red dressed up in a wicker-covered flask would have summed up old-style Chianti; but not any more. Gone is the gut-rot, gone (almost) are the expensive, folksy wicker flasks. Now after a concerted clean-up operation, most Chianti is either good and good value, or very good and very good value. The red Sangiovese grape is mainly responsible for this wine, helped along by other varieties both red and white, plus some 'optional extras' including none other than good old Cabernet Sauvignon. Seven specific sub-districts compose the Chianti area, with Chianti Classico being the most important and responsible for most of the best wines. Chianti Rufina is another distinguished name to find on the label. If the wine simply calls itself Chianti, it may come from a blend of grapes grown anywhere in the whole area, and in the hands of a good wine-maker, that's no bad thing.

Straightforward Chianti is at its lively best drunk young, when it may even be served slightly chilled. It then has vibrant – almost fizzy – fruit and a soft dustiness. You'll find plums in there, tart skins and all, and hints of cherries, too. But the most unusual taste trigger for this wine is a distinct aroma of tea, like the lingering scent of the wet leaves left in the bottom of the pot. Taste more closely, and you'll find hints of pepper as you swallow. In the Classico versions, this pepper is more like spice and the fruit weightier and more succulent. The legendary way to serve this wine is with pasta – but it goes with virtually every other non-fish Italian dish, too; not at its best served without food, though.

Corvo/Sicily

Sicily produces a host of good things in the wine line, but by far the best known is Corvo, not a place, not a grape but, for once, a brand name used for precise wines made from precise grape varieties (all obscure and Sicilian). Making wines in hot Mediterranean climates presents the wine-maker (the thinking wine-maker, that is) with a dilemma. If he lets the grapes do what comes naturally to them, he gets strong, 'typical' wines which are hard to love. If he unleashes all the might of new technology on his brew, he knocks out their heart and their soul. Where Corvo (and Regaleali, another very good Sicilian wine to look out for) score trumps, is that they steer a clever middle course.

The Rosso, which is best at three to four years old, mixes the enticing flavours of ripe red fruits (blackberries principally) with the southern twang of leather, meat, stewed fruit and minerals. The Bianco (which should be drunk as young as possible) has a delicate fruit perfume and gentle almondy tinge to the taste. Both are welcome finds on a poor Italian wine list – you know exactly what you are going to get (and won't be disappointed – unless the white is too old, in which case reject it before they remove the cork).

Dolcetto

Like Barbera, this is a grape variety which lends its name to no fewer than seven different wines, all from different places; the places forming the other half of the name as in Dolcetto d'Alba, the best known example.

Dolce, of course, means sweet, but this red wine doesn't entirely live up to its name; it's the grapes themselves that are sweet, and that's *before* they were vinified. (You'll remember that during fermentation the yeast eats up the sugar and turns it into alcohol.) This wine is actually very dry, but there is compensation for you if you were expecting sweetness; the fruit is packed so densely into the flavour that you could be persuaded to believe there is a bit of sweetness there. Now, here's the riddle: how exactly would you describe the fruit? Berries? Some sort of berry fruit, but which one? It seems none precisely fits the description, but I'll tell you something, if such a fruit did actually exist, we'd all be wolfing down punnets of it. It's a very alluring taste indeed. In true Italian style, there's a vibrance to the taste, too, sparked off by keen

acidity, at its most pronounced in young wines. A middleweight among reds, best served with uncomplicated, even bland food – try it with macaroni or cauliflower cheese – and at room temperature.

Frascati

This is Rome's white wine, made from grapes grown on the great ridge of hills south-east of the city where influential Romans (including the Pope) have their summer homes. The Malvasia and Trebbiano grape varieties are behind this once yellow wine; with the smartening up of vinification practices, though, the colour has simmered down to a paler shade and the quality and popularity have soared.

Because Frascati may be made entirely from one or other of its grapes, or from a mixture of both, there's no typical style. The spectrum of tastes ranges from a nutty, creamy, apricot medley at the heavy-on-Malvasia end of the scale, down to a clean, steely, almost sharp style if the wine is Trebbiano-led. *Aficionados* **generally go for the Malvasia style (look out for Colli di Catone or Villa Catone wines), but whichever type you end up with get it as young as possible and serve it well chilled. In Rome they pull the cork of a Frascati no matter what is on the menu – fish, meat, cheese, the lot – and it's generally considered that the Romans know a thing or two about partnering food and wine.**

Gavi

Buzz wine of the eighties, Gavi has been lucky enough for its great popularity in Italy to have spread to the great fashion-led wine market of America. It's a funny little white wine, this, and I really can't see what all the fuss is about. It comes from a small area a few miles north of Genoa and is made from the local Cortese grape.

At worst, it's nothing much to write about – home, or anywhere – being rather nondescript. But find a good one and you'll discover it has great delicacy. There's a floweriness on the bouquet which goes on to suggest rose petals in the flavour – occasionally as intense as a fragrant sachet for your underclothes drawer. But there's a firmness and a crispness to it, too, with lemony hints cutting through the

creaminess. Underneath it all (if there is an 'all', that is) it is an extremely dry wine, though, and to benefit from the 'added flavours' you need to give it time to develop – at least a couple of years after the vintage, when it tastes very bonny on a hot summer's day with smoked salmon, seafood or chicken salad. Don't overchill.

Lambrusco

Fizzy fun wine. Lambrusco comes in any shade you like. That's not how it started out, though: in its native Emilia Romagna around Modena, north-west of Bologna, it developed almost by accident. Lambrusco is the local red grape, and had to take second place in the agricultural calendar to the production of Parmesan cheese and Parma ham. So if the cold weather struck before the wine had fully fermented, it would numb the yeasts and prevent them from finishing their job. So the wine would be bottled active yeast and all . . . and come the spring, the yeast would work again and the resultant gas would be trapped to add fizz to the wine. Traditionally Lambrusco was all red and all dry – really quite searingly so – and became accepted as the perfect wine to accompany the rich Bologna food. But giving it an international appeal, gradually the sweet style we know and love appeared, quickly followed by the other shades of white and pink.

Red   This is the real thing – it has more going for it than the others (and is the authentic colour after all). When it is first poured, it looks like Ribena with a beer head on it, beautiful purply red with bags of white froth. This is splendidly fruity wine in a cherryade sort of way – adult soda pop is one way of looking at it. But it's not all that frivolous; it can play a serious role at the dinner table teamed especially with Italian salami and spicy sausages. Best of all is the dry style, generally called Tradizione on the label.

White   May or may not be made from the grape of the same name and is generally an emasculated version of the red.

Rosé   In my experience the rosés are terrifically variable in quality, ranging from poor to less good than the reds.

Lugana

Unheard of in Britain until the last few years, this Lake Garda peach is now quite the thing. Although it comes from the ubiquitous white Trebbiano grape (responsible for all sorts of bland monstrosities), it is from a peculiar clone of the same, which lifts it cork and shoulders above the rest.

So, for this particular variation on a theme, you have the same gentle, creamy base, but this time overlaid with walnuts, Cox's apples, a hint of fresh pear, a smidgen of orange peel and a touch of liquorice. When the wine's brand new (jump on it as soon as it hits the shelves in the spring following the year of its harvest) the acidity is up and raring to go, giving the wine a positive energy charge. By the time the next spring approaches, the acidity has softened to have become hardly noticeable; this spells the end of the wine – and announces the imminent arrival of the next vintage.

Merlot

Red 'party Merlot' in big cheap bottles won't actually thrill, but it'll serve the purpose. No prizes for guessing the grape (Bordeaux's Merlot, of course), vinified inexpensively in the Veneto region in the north-east.

Surprisingly at the price, you can detect some sort of grape character, the comforting fruit cake flavours of Merlot flickering through the perky acidity so characteristic of Italian reds. There's also a grassiness in there, a typical flavour found in most reds from the north-east. The fruitiness is somewhat short-lived; it's fine as far as it goes, though, and who'll notice, if it's a good party?

Montepulciano d'Abruzzo

This red wine really gives you a taste of Italy at its best. Montepulciano is the grape, Abruzzo the place, the large region stretching for seventy or so miles down the Adriatic coast and back into the centre of the country to the high peaks of the Apennine backbone. And seldom does the combination fail.

The intense, vivid purple colour warns that this wine is going to be packed with deep dense flavour, and it is! There's a marvellous ripe bramble medley in there, combining the scents and flavours of blackberries and cranberries with a swipe of tart fruity acidity. This zippy acidity is a classic feature

of Italian red wines, giving them an unmistakable surge of liveliness, and preventing the fruit from getting out of hand and becoming altogether too soft and jammy. No, this wine is bone dry, has enough essential tannin (the element that makes your mouth feel dry) to give it grip, and ends on a firm peppery and spicy note that makes it a great food wine – red meat being the best partner.

Orvieto

At first sight, the most remarkable thing about Orvieto, north of Rome, is its highly decorated cathedral. Until recently, visitors wouldn't have given the wine of the place a second thought, and that's not just because they were blinded by the beauty of the cathedral. It simply didn't deserve it, being middling sweet and dull. But wines from all over Italy have pulled themselves up by their boot straps and Orvieto has made a big (and necessary) effort to do better. The ubiquitous Trebbiano is the major grape in volume terms for this white wine, but it is the Grecheto that adds the style. Classico versions are likely to be the best.

Most Orvieto is dry now – and that's what you expect from a bottle that doesn't tell you otherwise. Basically the wine is gentle and creamy, but overlaid on top of that, thanks to the Grecheto, are high points on the nutty flavour scale, suggesting almonds, hazel and walnuts plus the green fruit flavours of apples, pears and greengages. And if that sounds a lot going on in one wine, don't worry, it's still soft and very approachable at heart; good for summer patio drinking or to combine with flavoursome sauces coating fish and white meats.

Pinot Grigio

The Italian version of the Pinot Gris in France, this grape proliferates in the north-east of the country where it produces white wines ranging from the limp and lily-livered to smart, interesting, unusual treats. Friuli is the best area – look out for it on the label either just above or just below the grape.

Cheap examples can seem rather concocted, with a slug of apparently overlaid acidity tagged on to a dismally uninteresting wine. But the better (usually higher priced) examples can be intriguing, to say the least. Picture the scene in the glass! There you have hints of sunflower or refined olive oil coupled

with memories of freshly cooked fish. Look further
and you may spy kumquats, marzipan and nuts.
Put all these seemingly disparate (and unlikely)
flavours together, and you have a good, well-
rounded taste in your mouth. This wine is not
designed to be tackled too young – wait until it has a
year or two's maturity to it for it to show off its best –
when it makes a good partner to . . . fish fried in oil
followed by kumquats and nuts!

Soave

Just east of the Romeo and Juliet city of Verona is the little
hilltop village of Soave, giving its name to one of Italy's
best known white wines. The slopes radiating down from
the village are occupied by the best vineyards which go to
make the best wines (earmarked as Classico) while more
ordinary quality – millions of litres of the stuff to meet
world demand – is produced from the plains below.
Garganega is the main grape variety which, with some
Trebbiano, goes to make this reliably okay wine, concealing few surprises or excitements. A good producer to look
out for is Zenato.

There are no sparks here, think more in terms of
fresh easy drinking white wine and you won't be
disappointed. You'll notice a creamy nuttiness to
the taste once you get past the slightly bland
bouquet, like freshly blanched almonds which turn
into bitter almonds as you swallow, leaving your
mouth revived and refreshed. Youth is the watch-
word, the younger the better, so seek out the new
wines as they come on stream in the spring (bearing
the date of the previous year's harvest) and stick
with them until the next batch of new wines comes
along the next spring. Older Soaves are best
avoided, being rather flat and boring.

Teroldego Rotaliano

An idiosyncrasy from the plains of Rotaliano in the north-
east, this red wine is born of the local Teroldego grape.
Not exactly born to make great things though . . . but
acceptable ones at least.

Reds from the north-east tend to be grassy, lean,
rather short on flavour and a little dusty-dry in the
mouth. Teroldego is no exception. But get a good
one with enough fruit to last the course and you'll
find some satisfying redcurrant flavours spiked
with white pepper and allspice.

Tocai

To be confused with neither Tokay d'Alsace nor the cara-mel-sweet Tokay from Hungary, Tocai is an Italian grape variety in its own right, and makes interesting enough cheap white plonk inland from Venice and on round to Trieste.

Styles vary quite a bit, but in general the price will reflect the quality quite accurately: the cheaper it is, the more wishy-washy it will be. Taste triggers for this wine revolve around fig and greengage flavours with a bit of apple, but you have to search for them, they're not all that strong. You may also find a touch of nutty creaminess and a faint tang of aniseed. At the right price, served good and cold, they are economical party wines – and provide enough interest to take you through the whole evening.

Trebbiano

In the big league of white grape varieties, Trebbiano (alias Ugni Blanc) comes high in quantity, and almost as low as you can get in terms of character and class. It does work quite successfully blended with other more interesting sorts; but on its own, it would require too much discipline, too much expense to make creating interesting wines a viable option. The commonest wine with the grape on the label is Trebbiano d'Abruzzo, where it is actually blended with another grape variety, locally called Trebbiano d'Abruzzo. (Things are never as simple as they seem.)

Although it can rise to dizzy heights where quinces and tropical fruits seem to have a hand in the taste medley, Trebbiano d'Abruzzo doesn't usually soar. Generally it is light and simple with a bitter after-taste. Okay, if dead cold and liberally dished up on a hot summer's day, perhaps with a plate of delicate risotto.

Valpolicella

North of Verona you find the 'valley of many cellars' – Val pol i cella (actually series of valleys is more to the point) – producing light glugging red wine that has been in danger of being spoilt by its success. The best vineyards are sited on the upland areas and their grapes go to make the best Classico wines (worth looking out for – the extra expendi-ture pays off). Ordinary Valpol has always relied on the less spectacular vineyards on the valley floors, and pushed

by hectic world-wide demand for this wine, the area covered by these has grown . . . and grown, and quality has suffered accordingly. A veritable cocktail of grapes goes to make this world famous wine, with Corvina being the most important.

Age has a considerable effect on Valpolicella (as I suppose, it does on us all); and, unusually for a classic red wine, the general rule here is the younger the better. Young Valpolicella drunk from the spring following the harvest (the previous year's date) can be a treat – especially served chilled – conjuring up a marvellous surge of alcohol-steeped cherries. Unfortunately this style is not the most usual. Traditional producers hold much store in ageing the wine in large oak barrels and selling it at two or three years old. However, what they fail to notice is that their wine is usually too lily-livered to stand up to the lengthy ageing process, and all too often it arrives knackered on our shelves. Good gutsy older Valpolicella, however, adds smoky, leathery, even chocolatey notes to the cherry medley.

Amarone della Valpolicella (formerly called Recioto della Valpolicella Amarone) is made from the best grapes which are picked and left on racks to dry, so concentrating the juice. And the resultant wine is robust, to say the least, and lives up to its name – amarone = the big bitter. Bitterness is not all, however; there's a super-concentration of cherry fruit flavours as well. Not a wine to be tackled lightly; it's a serious undertaking to open a bottle of Amarone. A wine simply called Recioto della Valpolicella is sweet.

Verdicchio

The first thing you notice about Verdicchio is the shapely amphora bottle – in Italy, for obvious reasons, called 'La Lollobrigida'. And it used to be the only thing, since the contents were thoroughly unremarkable. Verdicchio is the white grape variety, and Jesi inland from Ancona on the Adriatic coast, the town around which the vineyards sprawl. So to give it its full name it is known as Verdicchio dei Castelli di Jesi (*castelli* being castles). The best wines are the Classico ones.

Like so many of its poor relations, Verdicchio is becoming richer, at least in quality. But it is still essentially simple stuff, generally at its best young

and fresh when it is crisp, clean and dry with a salty-minerally-metallic edge. Better wines – often from individual vineyard sites (they will make their presence felt on the label) – are fuller and richer with better defined memories-of-the-sea saltiness. The Adriatic's answer to Muscadet, Verdicchio is most at home washing down plates of seafood and fish.

Vermentino di Sardegna

The introduction of high tech wine-making techniques had the effect of a crash diet in Sardinia, alias Sardegna. From big, fat, alcoholic usually sweet white thunderbolts, her mainstream wines transformed themselves into slim, delicate little things, to the delight of British wine buyers. Vermentino is the grape grabbing most of the action so far.

Don't stop to examine this wine too long! It is ideal for quaffing back without a care, being mouth-wateringly fresh and lowish in alcohol. If you do give it time to say something to you, its conversation will revolve around a piercing acidity, spiking the vital fruit and giving the bite of a sweet-sharp apple, a dash of grapefruit juice or a nip of just ripe gooseberry. The younger the better, the cooler the better and away you go.

Vernaccia di San Gimignano

Three completely different grape varieties go by the name Vernaccia – probably because it roughly means 'belonging to here' . . . there and everywhere. The most often seen, though, is the Vernaccia di San Gimignano, named after the medieval town of that name in Tuscany. And lately this white wine has taken two great steps, one forwards, and the other back. Let me explain. New technology in the wine cellar ironed out some of the less likeable traits of old – the yellowness, the flabbiness, the oxidation which we had all long since tired of – but it was felt flushed out most of the flavour with it. So a step backwards was necessary to retrieve some of the old character by loosening up the grip of the antiseptic new methods. A balancing act has now been performed.

There's a hint of buzzy Chardonnay character to the best of these wines which can be almost buttery. But there's a jab of un-Chardonnay-like citrus acidity to them as well, almost a salty-steely tang. Underneath it all, and fusing all the other elements

together, is the definite flavour of brazil nuts. But don't be surprised if the first few sips slip down hardly being noticed at all. These restrained subtle flavours take time to assert themselves – and regrettably if you have a second-rate bottle, they probably never will.

Vino Nobile di Montepulciano

Don't take everything you read at face value . . . there's nothing particularly noble about most wines going by this name, and the Montepulciano part is quite unrelated to the Montepulciano in Montepulciano d'Abruzzo. In Abruzzo it is a grape variety, here, it is a hilltop town in southern Tuscany. So that sorts that out. The official Chianti area, although concentrated further north, drifts down to surround the Montepulciano enclave, and as both red wines are made from much the same sort of grapes, not surprisingly there is a resemblance in taste, too.

Plums and prunes, that's what first springs out of a glass of this stuff, along with the piercing scent of morello cherries steeped in alcohol . . . and a waft of black weak tea. There are concentrated flavours in there, at their most acute when the wine is between two and four years old. Taste the same wine from five to ten years old and you get a much more subdued, elegantly restrained view of the whole thing.

Germany

THERE HAS BEEN a long-standing mutual admiration society between British tastes and German wines. Historically the favourite style of the British has been white, light and medium dry, precisely the identikit picture of accessibly priced German wines. Liebfraumilch has been the Farley's rusk among wines; in Britain, when first being introduced to wine, more people have cut their teeth on Liebfraumilch than on any other wine style. And very appropriately, too, since it is simple, easy drinking stuff.

Such has been Britain's affinity with Germany's cheap and cheerful white wines that it has largely cornered the market on them, bagging greater volumes than any other country in the world. Germany has relied on Britain as her premier export market, but she hadn't bargained for the fickle finger of fashion and whim. Slowly the British are turning their backs on their old favourites and looking elsewhere for their cheap and easy thrills. Liebfraumilch has taken something of a nose dive in popularity and Germany is now exploring other ways of winning British custom.

Curiously, although Germany puts out massive volumes of easy drinking 'medium' white wine, it's far from her strongest point. Germany's forte is in producing fine wines – among the finest dry, medium and sweet wines in the world. But these wines have enjoyed only minuscule success in Britain, in part because their labels are so incredibly indigestible. The gothic script is often off-putting for a start, and that is before you try to tackle the unappetisingly long-winded way the wines describe themselves. But, but, but *at last* the problem has been recognised and attempts are being made to make everything a bit simpler to try to lure back the disillusioned customer.

So now the new wave German wines are taking two new routes. One is to name themselves simply after grape varieties (in ordinary writing, no frills and serifs) and to present themselves in commonplace wine bottles so they don't even look German any more. And the other is to play up the fact that Germany produces dry wines as well. The slide away from the old easy drinking light 'n' sweetish favourites from Germany has been partly towards Italy's Lambrusco (now the best selling wine in the world), which is taking over in Britain as the new Farley's rusk. But it has also been partly towards drier wines. For a while now, sweet has not been considered chic. Dry white wine is the thing and Germany is bending over backwards to prove that she, too, does a good line in crisp dry whites; well worth looking out for, identified on the label as either trocken or simply dry.

In Germany, wines have traditionally been considered rather differently from how they are viewed elsewhere. Until recently, most people around the world thought of wine as a drink to serve with food. In Britain, beer or gin and tonic and the like would traditionally have been drunk before the meal and wine (only on high days and holidays, perhaps) with it. But in Germany things were different. There it was wine that was the pleasure you sipped without the distraction of food, with friends before or after the meal, and it was beer, their other national drink, that was served with the grub. Germany has always principally been a white wine producing country (she doesn't have the right climate to put out serious red wines, although those that she makes can be refreshingly delicate and light).

So a particularly delicate flavour of wine, subtly scented, light and low in alcohol with a soothing dose of residual sugar was encouraged; the tartness and might needed to combat a solid dish of sauerkraut and wurst being encouraged in beer. And still the aperitif – and even digestif, if you eat early enough – role is best suited to the fruity, fragrant style of German wines, while the drier styles being made in increasing numbers and found in growing volumes in Britain are equally suited as wines to serve with delicate food.

Although simplicity is seen as the way forward for the flagging German wine market, regrettably the far-from-simple classification system still exists. Just to put you fully in the picture when you peer at these new straightforward wine labels, I must give you a brief résumé of the legal hierarchy among wines. Because Germany is perched right on the edge of the 'suitable-for-growing-grapes' latitude (a couple of steps further north and the weather would be too cool), sun is the most highly prized element in the vineyard, and so the quality classification for German wines revolves around the amount of sun that smiled on the grapes before they were picked. So in general the riper and sweeter the grapes when harvested, the more concentrated are the flavours and the better quality will be the resultant wine.

Just to complicate matters a bit further, though, this does not necessarily mean that the better the wine, the sweeter it will be. In the bottom quality categories it is permitted to add sweet grape juice back into the wine to sweeten it up, so you can get a very sweet *Deutscher Tafelwein*, for instance. It is also possible to make a really dry wine from very sweet juice, as they do in most other parts of the world. So ripeness here is linked principally to quality and only sometimes to style.

At the bottom of the quality scale comes *Deutscher Tafelwein*. It's important to look out for the word Deutscher – something simply called Tafelwein is probably a real old mongrel wine blended from anywhere in the EC and positively not recommended. This is ordinary table wine from virtually anywhere within Germany's eleven wine-producing regions. *Landwein* is a bit better, and legally supposed to be in a drier style. The next rung up the ladder is the biggest category of all and that is *Qualitätswein* (now wait for it) *bestimmte Anbaugebiete* or *QbA*. This is the best of the ordinary wines and must come from a more specific place and be able to prove to the authorities that it is more individual in style.

Qualitätswein mit Prädikat (*QmP* for short) literally means quality wine with special attributes, and within this general 'fine wine' category there are six distinct quality ratings with different attributes, the grapes becoming riper and so the flavours concentrating as you go progressively up the quality scale. The lowliest of the Prädikats is *Kabinett* which is likely to be lower in alcohol than a QbA wine and, indeed, than any other full strength wine in the world, because at this quality level the fermentation must rely entirely on the sugar naturally present in the grapes and not, as is the case in the lower quality classes, be boosted by added sugar. Kabinett wines are therefore very light, delicate and subtly scented.

Next up is *Spätlese* meaning 'late picked', the grapes being of sufficiently good quality to be able to stay on the vines for at least seven days after the normal harvest to enable them to build up higher reserves of sugar. In this category there can be enough natural sugar in the juice for some to be left in the wine once the fermentation has been completed so contributing natural sweetness; alternatively it may all be fermented out to make a full flavoured dry wine. In lower quality wines the sweetness generally derives from the addition of sweet grape juice to the wine. *Auslese* is made from selected bunches of the best (i.e. sweetest) grapes to make intense wines bursting with aromas and packed with flavour, either lusciously sweet or, more fashionably, dry.

Beerenauslese is made from sweet, individually selected grapes which may have had their sugar content concentrated by a special mould visiting the vines in the best years. This is concentratedly sweet wine, though less so than the intensely rich, sweet and honeyed *Trockenbeerenauslese* which is made only in the very best years from specially selected mould-attacked grapes. Trockenbeeren means 'dry berry' grapes, because they are picked (individually) when they are almost raisin-like. *Eiswein* is an oddity, an intensely sweet wine made from grapes picked so late that they have been frozen by frost, so concentrating the sugar.

As far as grapes are concerned, although Germany has been active in crossing vines to develop new varieties to flourish in her northerly conditions, as yet nothing has been found to surpass the Riesling for the best wines and the Müller-Thurgau, itself a relatively new crossing, for producing volumes of easy drinking hooch. Technically, though, each grape variety or blend of grape varieties may make wine capable of achieving any of the Prädikat classes. But since it is a great challenge in such a cool place to get grapes to ripen sufficiently to pack in the required amount of sugar to make the top wines, wine-makers don't tend to fool about with the work-horse grapes or the newly developed crossings at this level. Top quality German wines will always declare on the label from which grape variety they are made. In traditional wines in the ordinary Qualitätswein class (such as Piesporter Michelsberg), this is not customarily the case. But the new breed of varietal wines, nearly all Qualitätsweins, shout the grape type loud and clear on the label, and you'll find some unusual names cropping up. (You'll also, incidentally, find the new German grape varieties mentioned on labels of English wine; many of our own wine-makers take their lead from Germany.)

If, starting with Qualitätswein (and concentrating on a single grape variety) you were to taste your way through all the quality classifications, you'd find that the bottom rung would probably be quite broad and possibly fairly sweet. Up to Kabinett and the body would thin out considerably, the wine would be very delicate and the scents and flavours become finely tuned and elusive. At the Spätlese level, you'd get more body and concentration of flavour and in a traditional style wine (as opposed to a new wave Trocken) a richer sense of sweetness. Auslese takes you up into yet more concentration and probably silkier, more evident sweetness (though there would certainly be a good prickle of acidity, too, to balance out). Beerenauslese and Trockenbeerenauslese are the real sweeties, the most luscious, viscous, intensely honeyed tastes you could find in a glass – but still retaining the lively acidity and the beautifully perfumed bouquet for which fine German wines are renowned.

Now a look at the grapes most widely used and their tastes in German wines.

The Grapes and Their Taste:

Kerner

Like Müller-Thurgau, this white grape was developed from a Riesling cross with the intention of getting better yields. Like the Riesling, it can be harvested late when more sugar has packed into the grapes, and so adapts well to making the higher qualities of wine in good years.

There is an aromatic spiciness to the Kerner, and it can have a healthy stab of acidity, too, but still tends to be a bit bland. Plantings are on the up, however.

Morio-Muskat

Despite its Muskat name (and character), this white grape is no relation of the Muscat of Alsace, Asti Spumante *et al*. It's actually a cross between Silvaner and Pinot Blanc (Weisser Burgunder) – though bears little or no resemblance to either.

It's a loud-mouthed grape if ever I met one, shouting its pungent, spicy, grapey flavours loud and clear. There's the rich scent of pawpaws and mangoes on the nose, married to big, fat sultanas. The flavour is mouth-fillingly grapey and so powerfully scented and flavoured it almost seems artificial – like a tin of Parma violet sweets with a slight plastic edge. The fruit and spice carry with them an apparent sweetness, even if the wine is quite dry. It is now sometimes vinified into a single variety wine – marvellous as an introduction to non-wine drinkers (and as a partner for Oriental food) and is also used in small measure as a blending wine. A little goes a long way.

Müller-Thurgau

This high yielding, easy to grow white grape is by far the most popular with German wine growers, who have planted it over vast areas of each of the eleven wine-growing regions.

It is a pungent grape, offering simultaneously scents of flowers, fruit and spice. Get into the taste, and you'll find the acidity is low so the wine tends to have little thrust, but continues in a soft, easy-going spicy, cinnamon-scented way, frothing over with simple, sweet, sugary lychee and kiwi fruit flavours. The flavour of boiled sweets never seems to be far away and at the end of the mouthful you can have that catch in the back of the throat – as though you've had too many boiled sweets.

Riesling

Nowhere in the world is the Riesling so highly revered as it is in Germany – and with good reason. In the 'marginal' (as far as grape growing is concerned) vineyards of Germany the grape struggles to produce some of the most highly praised white wines in the world. And as we have discussed, these may range from searingly dry to unctuously sweet. But no matter what the level of residual sugar in the wine, the Riesling hangs on tightly to its own individuality.

There is a floweriness to the bouquet of Riesling wines, conjuring up visions of the most delicately scented alpine flowers, and even freesias. Both on the bouquet and in the taste there is a suggestion of oiliness, a petrolly connotation reminiscent of an aeroplane revving up – or camphor, if you've ever dabbled with model steam trains – and a silky feel, too. Acidity is always vibrant, making the mouth water as it does for a juicy green apple, spiking the scented taste. There can be a suggestion of new mown grass too, and even a faint, albeit finely tuned earthiness.

Scheurebe

Scheurebe is a successful 'son of Riesling' which makes delicious quality white wines up to Spätlese class.

The taste triggers here are flowering currants and grapefruit – the grapefruit coming from the grapes' naturally high acidity.

Silvaner

A potentially bland variety, Silvaner is responsible for making slightly coarse, neutral white wines, possibly with a muddy, vegetal quality. It used to be the most widely planted variety in Germany, but has been easily overtaken by the Müller-Thurgau now.

Vinified as a single varietal, you can find a slight nuttiness on the bouquet and a suggestion of pomegranates and passion-fruit in the taste. The flavour of apricot kernels may strike you, too, and a faint peachy quality. More often it is used to blend with other varieties, where it can add gumption to a wine that would otherwise be too slight and lily-livered.

Weisser Burgunder

This is Germany's name for France's Pinot Blanc and Italy's Pinot Bianco. Although little is planted in Germany, it is making its presence felt on British wine shelves where it is seen as a single variety, invariably in the dry, or trocken, style. Plantings in Germany are concentrated in Baden and the Rheinpfalz – the two areas nearest to France's Alsace – but it seems to behave quite differently on the other side of the Rhine.

In Germany, it can smack of canned lychees, pretending it's going to be sweet, but in fact being quite surprisingly dry. There can be the merest suggestion of Jerusalem artichokes to it as well. Otherwise it has a creamy lemony character and a silky texture.

The Best-known Wines:

The names of the grapes will be found on new style German wines simply named after individual grape varieties. These tend to be of the simple Qualitätswein quality. Fancier wines in the Prädikat classes also frequently name the grape variety behind the wine – which if it is a traditional wine, will be increasingly sweet the further you climb up the quality ladder. However, the German wines most commonly found in Britain are named not after a grape, but after an area. Frequently these are commercial spin-offs to some highly respected fine wine from an individual vineyard, which took the name in vain many decades ago, and became pot boilers in their own right. Here are taste profiles of the most widely found 'generic' German wines.

Bereich Bernkastel

A bereich is a collection of a collection of vineyards (the smaller collection being called a grosslage and having its own group name). Bereich Bernkastel in the Mosel has three grosslagen, among them the famous Piesporter Michelsberg and the occasionally seen Bereich Kurfurstlay.

If you're lucky, this white wine should give you a hint of the Mosel flavour, being delicate, having a noticeable appley acidity and giving a slight sherbety feel on the tongue. You may find hints of stewed apples, kiwi fruits and boiled sweets in the flavour – and the curious fleeting aroma of card-board boxes with their sweet glue. Müller-Thurgau is the most likely grape behind the blend, but look out for examples boasting the Riesling grape as they'll be more distinguished. As with all German wines, this benefits from being served good and cool and can be served as an aperitif, German style. or to accompany any delicate white meat or fish dishes. It is also good with seafood if you're looking for a soft, medium dry companion.

Ihr		Hessische Bergstrasse
Mittelrhein		Baden
Mosel-Saar-Ruwer		Württemberg
Rheingau		Franken
Nahe		
Rheinhessen		
Rheinpfalz		

Hock Deutscher Tafelwein

Queen Victoria is alleged to have coined the name Hock as a shortening for Hochheim, source of her favourite wines in the Rheingau. It has now come to mean wine from any one of four regions – most likely Rheinhessen and Rheinpfalz. Although a basic quality white wine, you could do worse.

There'll inevitably be a pungent, floral nose to it – tinged with a ferrous, rusty edge sometimes (a bit like the smell of old batteries). But sadly, it could well lack acidity and so appear to be very flabby and purposeless and simply downright dull. The sweetness can tend to taste rather 'added on' and unnatural, giving a nyeuk (if you know what I mean) taste once you have swallowed, which can linger on. I certainly wouldn't like to stick on this one for a whole evening, but a quick glass straight from the fridge is all right. As with all modest qual-ity German wines, it should be drunk as young as possible (so don't leave a bottle lying around for long before opening it).

Liebfraumilch

Of all the plagiarisms found in the naming of German wines, this one takes the biscuit. A small vineyard near Worms in the Rheinhessen called Liebfrauenkirche (Church of Our Lady) made – and still does, look out for it – pretty okay wine, and was known for it. Some bright spark had the idea of calling a wine Liebfraumilch (the milk of Our Lady) and flogging it to Britain, to become the biggest selling wine in the country – and for a time, virtually any wine could call itself this made-up name Liebfraumilch. The rules were tightened recently, and now the wine must come from the Rheinhessen, Rheinpfalz, the Nahe or the Rheingau (ha ha) and be made from either Riesling, Silvaner, Müller-Thurgau or Kerner. In practice, though, since Liebfraumilch earned itself a reputation for being Germany's cheapest offering on the shelves, standards have not been that great. It is essentially Germany's cheapest plonk (and remarkably, virtually unknown in Germany, being an entirely British phenomenon).

To taste, you'd be very unlucky not to have a suggestion of Germany's tempting floweriness somewhere in the bouquet or flavour, although like as not it'll be crowded out by less welcome characteristics such as tartness, sourness, hints at stale milk, sulphur and an overwhelming sense of tedium. In my experience, the most interesting examples come from the Nahe (look for this on the label). Unless you have a good one you're devoted to, I'd be inclined to experiment with something else.

Mosel Deutscher Tafelwein

Of the Tafelweins, this white is likely to be the best bet. The Mosel is a comparatively small wine-producing area, with frequently very difficult to manage vineyard sites on precipitous slopes, so in general the standards are higher (or should I rephrase that, are less likely to sink so low).

Even a humble beast like this can give you a flavour of the Mosel with a sharp piercing scent of gooseberries (toned down with suggestions of boiled sweets). As it's only modest quality, the sweetness does not always appear to be integral; so the wine can have a dry bouquet and a syrupy thickly sweet taste. This must be rescued by a good prickle of acidity (a strong point of Mosel wines) which will temper down the slightly acrid after-taste.

Niersteiner Gutes Domtal

Gutes Domtal is a collection of vineyards in the region of Nierstein (Rheinhessen) with the yet larger catchment of collections of vineyards being Bereich Nierstein, which also appears on some labels. Both white wines are much of a muchness in quality terms and are capable (as are all other catch-all names of German wines) of harbouring a multitude of sins, partly because they try to be too cheap for their own good. Germany has carved out the bottom notch of any price scale to her cost.

Although you may find inviting spring flower hints on the bouquet, perhaps an attractive edge of cinnamon and spice, there's certain to be something lacking somewhere. Often these wines seem unfinished. They start well on the nose, but then are unable to fulfil their promise, seeming coarse and sugary, flabbily lacking acidity and perhaps rather vegetably. The acrid taste that crops up again often goes hand in hand with an unfinished taste, a yeastiness that shouldn't be there. If you feel a catch in your throat, or a tickling in your nose that makes you sneeze – that's too high a sulphur content; another common fault in overly cheap wines.

Piesporter Michelsberg

This old favourite from the Mosel can be good and can be very poor. The austerity of the Mosel style, steely acidity and so youthfully green and unripe it almost hurts, is captured in this popular white and, if all goes well and it is balanced by a hint of flowers or even spice, then all well and good. If not, it can be as unfriendly as tripping over in a patch of nettles; sharp and edgy and at times (when the sulphur is too high) downright uncomfortable.

Trocken

Trocken simply means dry, and to shout loud and clear what they are about, some Qualitätsweins are now simply called 'Trocken', and that is what they are. A pretty, delicately scented nose generally leads you into a simple, if rather wishy-washy, bland but dry white wine. Of the modestly priced German wines, the Trockens are the most natural partners for food – partnering anything you care to put with them bar hefty red meat dishes and concoctions heavy on pepper and spice.

Major Wine-producing Areas:

Germany's wines come from eleven different wine-producing areas clustered around the rivers Rhine and Mosel. To a lesser or greater extent, all but four of these areas export their wines to Britain, and the name of the region always appears on the label. Qualitätsweins come from a single region – and sometimes more precisely from a defined area or even vineyard within that region. Traditionally, wines from the Mosel come in green bottles and wines from the Rhine, brown. But with the flurry of new wines on the shelves afraid of Germany's rather tarnished image in the UK, all manner of shapes and colours are now being introduced in a bid for national anonymity.

Rheinhessen

The large, fertile undulating plane fringed to the north and east by the River Rhine (it turns a 90° corner at Mainz) is responsible for some of the best known wines available – and some of the dreariest. And regrettably these are one and the same. Although there is a plethora of obscure little wines made in this huge area, these remain virtually unknown. Why bother to paddle your own rickety canoe when you could simply hitch it to a provenly seaworthy lumbering great ocean liner? So reason the vast majority of the area's thousands of wine-makers. For the Rheinhessen is home of both Niersteiner and Liebfraumilch. Although the illustrious Nierstein name attached to that of a single vineyard promises a delicate, soft, flowery delight from the best riverfront vineyards around the town of that name, it has also been nabbed for use by just about any wine made in the surrounding hinterland covering a third of the whole huge Rheinhessen area. The other option open to a Rheinhessen wine producer is to call his wine Liebfraumilch, another highly popular catch-all name in the Qualitätswein class (see page 93). Other Rheinhessen wines you will see abounding on our shelves are varietal wines named after single grape varieties. Because there is a range of different soils and of microclimates in this large area, a multitude of new-crossing grape varieties are planted here, as well as the tried and tested Müller-Thurgau, Silvaner and Riesling.

Rheinpfalz

From south of the Rheinhessen running down to the French border, you find Germany's biggest producer, the 'Pfalz, falling into two distinct chunks, the north – producing some individual treats with their own charming, if sometimes rather saucy, personalities – and the mass-production south which, among other purposes, has Liebfraumilch very much in mind. The northern section of this wine-producing giant harbours some good names to look out for on the labels of fine German wines, including Deidesheim and Ruppertsberg. Riesling flourishes here and produces individually spicy wines heavily laden with exotic fruit scents and flavours. Traditionally Müller-Thurgau and Silvaner dominated the southern part, but these are now being nudged out in favour of the more highly aromatic, instantly nose thrilling new vine crossings. This is where the rush of single variety wines on our shelves generally come from.

Rheingau

This is the name to tweak the expectant taste buds of all Germany's greatest fans. You see, the Rhine trips along south to north to Mainz, when it takes a sharp left about turn and flows for a glorious stretch from east to west, leaving the vineyards of the Rheingau north of the river, basking on south-facing slopes on the sides of the Taunus hills, catching the rays not just from the sun, but also refracted from the water. So these are among the peachiest vineyards possible, where the Riesling ripens to wonderful, pot-pourri perfection offsetting the oily, grapey fullness with a ripple of racy fresh acidity. And not surprisingly, famous names jostle one another along the golden stretch, names such as Johannisberg (being so important as to be included, double-barrelled, in Riesling's name in the new world) and Hochheim (Queen Victoria is alleged to have coined the name Hock for Rhine wines from this village). The Rheingau is legally nominated as one of the permitted areas of production for Liebfraumilch, but in practice none comes from here, because there is no need to plough fine wine with the illustrious Rheingau pedigree and passport into an anonymous generic class (with a very mixed reputation).

Mosel-Saar-Ruwer

The precipitous slopes jack-knifing down to the windy Mosel (or Moselle, as it is often called) and its two tributaries the Saar and the Ruwer, as it twists and turns this way and that, are capable of producing Riesling at its greenest, streamlined best. And green is the trigger. Not only do Mosel wines come in green bottles, but the wine has that just-budded freshness, that lilt of lively acidity and faint prickly spritz that calls to mind this colour. Think of your tongue peppered with sherbet and imagine your nose in a bouquet of fresh-picked spring flowers – you're already in the Mosel mood. The best wines come from, and are named after, the best (of course) precipitous slopes. But again these names can be bastardised and grabbed by wines made in a much more general, much less propitious catchment area. So you have Bernkasteler Doctor being one of the most highly rated vineyards, producing Riesling at its most magnificent, and Bereich Bernkastel, having little in common bar the name, to which some 22 240 acres of vineyard on both sides of the river are entitled, much more likely concentrating on the work-horse grape Müller-Thurgau than on the noble, cussidly late ripening Riesling. And you have the famous village of Piesport giving its name to some venerable Rieslings . . . and, with the Michelsberg handle attached (showing the wine comes from a large collection of villages, rather than the one famous site), some fairly ordinary, bland 'medium' whites. Whether wines come from the Mosel or either of its tributaries, the wine is referred to as a Mosel or Moselle.

Nahe

The River Nahe with its accompanying valley runs north-west, parallel to the Mosel, to join the River Rhine at Bingen, and gives its name to a wine region renowned for its good value medium to excellent quality wines. Some of the yield makes its way into Liebfraumilch (the Nahe is one of the four legitimate sources), and good they are too; in the main, these Nahe Liebfraumilchs being a little more individual than the more usual examples from Rheinhessen and Rheinpfalz. Other Nahe wines found on our wine shelves tend to be individual wines from small producers some in the piquant, full, fruity aromatic style, others, away from the prime hilly slopes right in the centre of the region, tend to be blander, softer and less remarkable. The two catch-all names for ordinary quality wines are Schloss Böckelheim and Kreuznach. Predominating grape varieties are Müller-Thurgau, Riesling and Silvaner.

Baden

The stretched-out lozenge of Baden runs down beside the boundary with France to make Germany's most southerly wine region. This is Germany's Black Forest area, famous not just for cake, but for rather unusual wines as well (the grapes don't actually grow in the forest, of course). Here, in contrast to the other wine-producing zones, roughly a quarter of the grapes grown are red, principally Spätburgunder (alias Pinot Noir), which makes a surprisingly fiery red wine and a prettily fragrant rosé. The white wines are made from the ubiquitous Müller-Thurgau, as well as the fully flavoured Ruländer (alias Pinot Gris), spicy Gewürztraminer, soft, gentle Gutedel and, of course, the aristocratic Riesling. But what *really* makes these wines different is their surprisingly unGermanness. The drive to produce dry wines in Baden is longer established than in the other areas, and frequently there is a family resemblance in the best of these naturally higher strength wines with the neighbouring French wines of Alsace.

Franken

Far flung out towards the east along the River Main, the Franken vineyards have historically concentrated on producing dry wines in a no-nonsense, earthy style. Generally based on the work-horse grapes, the Silvaner and Müller-Thurgau, these are bottled in a Mateus Rosé-shaped squat bottle called a Bocksbeutel – and have a great following in their own country (the fashion for dry wines has a powerful grip in Germany, too) and so the few that are around tend to be a bit pricey.

Spain

SPANISH WINE HAS traditionally been a bit of a chameleon on its travels from home, changing image almost as often as the lizard does its colour. Sometimes the new hue has helped its appeal abroad; and sometimes it certainly hasn't.

First to make a show in Britain were the alarmingly cheap and dismal so-called Spanish Burgundies and Spanish Sauternes, so afraid of acknowledging their own roots, that they hid behind established French wine names instead, and managed to brainwash the public into believing that Spain was simply a producer of awful cheap plonk.

So when we were finally allowed a glimpse of what Spain could *really* do, with the introduction to our shelves of a selection of Riojas, it took quite a time for the wine-buying public to haul in the fact that, yes, Spain could produce wine, too, not merely cheap plonk. But slowly that message began to filter through; we accepted Rioja and liked it, but among class wines it stood alone. At the opposite end of the quality spectrum we were still meanwhile being bombarded by gut-rot, this time in the shape of the Big Brands.

The major brewery chains with their sights on their huge numbers of pubs and their large chains of off-licences, decided to market Spanish wines under a catch-all name such as Corrida (known in the trade for obvious reasons as Corroda) and Don Cortez. Okay, so Don Cortez had a major face-lift in the eighties and improved considerably, but by then the Great British Public had begun to move away from brands and to look more for individual wines with known pedigrees instead.

Spain, though, had failed to show us her 'other' pedigrees. Rioja had to wave the quality flag on its own. The problem was not simply with the marketing of Spanish wines in wine shops, it was actually more deep seated than that. The Spanish wine industry back at home was pretty old-fashioned as well. Lacking modern input of ideas and modern equipment, few producers were able to keep up with the times and those that did wanted to boast of their wines at home; there was a strong resistance to exporting her prized gems. When a Spanish wine (and it wasn't a Rioja) trounced all comers in the top class at the Paris wine olympics in 1979, people started to take note, not least the producers in Spain. All things became possible and the two horse race, consisting simply of Rioja and the Big Brands, was opened up to welcome representatives from all the other individual areas as well.

There are 35 *Denominaciónes de Origen*, that is officially demarcated quality wine-producing areas controlled by their own individual set of rules. By no means are all represented outside Spain – and even those that are, are as yet little recognised. Spain has a lot of catching up to do. But she now has the wines, and the desire to export them, and with luck is poised once again to change her image, this time to become accepted for the diverse and talented wine producer that she is. She is the third largest wine source in the world, and there's only one way for her to go now in terms of public perception, and that is up.

The Wines and Their Taste:

Cariñena

To the south-west of Rioja in Aragon, Cariñena has had the reputation for being a bit of a plonk producer in the past, sending her mighty, meaty alcoholic produce to the eager bars of Madrid. But there is a new verve down there for doing things well, and some surprisingly good things are now appearing on the shelves.

Red wines are the thing, and carefully made they can be splendidly up-front, liberally splashing their charms about with jammy sweet fruit and silky, oaky vanilla. Instantly likeable wines at generally instantly likeable prices.

Costers del Segre/Raimat

This most recent of Denominaciónes de Origen has sprung up round a tiny village giving its name to one of the most progressive bodegas in Spain. In the first edition of Hugh Johnson's famous *World Atlas of Wine* published in 1971, there's no mention of Raimat at all. In the updated '85 version, though, it is emblazoned across the map of Spain's north-east in whopping great bold black print. At the time of the first edition, there was no reason for Raimat to be included, sitting as it did in the middle of a desert. But big investment has changed the landscape more than somewhat, transforming this wasteland into a Garden of Eden for grapes. The first to be planted in this vinous health farm were the traditional Spanish varieties, and these were soon followed by the international favourites of Cabernet Sauvignon, Merlot and Chardonnay to complete the Raimat range. Marvellously concentrated, brash come-and-get-me scents and flavours leap out of these

thoroughly modern wines, all going under the Raimat label.

Abadia   This red is made from the Tempranillo combined with Cabernet Sauvignon, with a touch of Garnacho and Merlot added; a stunning international combination which gives the strong suggestion of summer pudding doused with double cream on the bouquet. And the taste to follow is no let-down either, having a voluptuous concentration of blackcurrant fruit.

Cabernet Sauvignon   The Cabernet Sauvignon is ripe and forward, spilling over with sweet blackcurrant scents and flavours, but also held back by a firm, solid backbone running through this red wine and preventing it from becoming too frivolous.

Tempranillo   Tempranillo is made into a single variety red wine of the same name, bursting with the rich scents of vanilla and pastry tweaked with a slight whiff of marsh marigolds, leading you into succulent fruity flavours. Easy drinking stuff as reds go, with bags of character to serve on its own, or as a versatile food wine – delicious with roast lamb and the works (including redcurrant jelly).

Chardonnay   The still Chardonnay shows the uncluttered peachy, lemony scents and flavours of the grape without the distraction of oak, although there's a breadth and depth you might not expect from a white wine made entirely in stainless steel.

La Mancha

The interminably flat, featureless plain of La Mancha, south of Madrid, where Don Quixote is fabled to have tilted at windmills (there are precious few of these left now) is Spain's wine-producing giant. Thirty per cent of all her vines are concentrated in this harsh, searingly hot, dry wilderness – and surprisingly, nine out of ten of these vines produces white grapes. The plucky little Airen vine copes best in these arid, extreme conditions, yielding grapes that go not only to make white wines, but also to calm down the might and main of the hot-climate reds. Traditionally, wine-producing co-operatives dominated production, buying grapes from about 20 000 growers with the incentive that the sweeter the grapes, the higher price they could command. And through the chemistry of wine-making, more sugar means higher alcohol, of course,

so the resultant wines were rather cumbersome and heavy-handed, to say the least. But they were cheap, and attractive to supermarket and high street wine chain buyers because of it. But here comes the interesting bit. For early in the eighties an unlikely thing happened; the British corporate wine buyers began to call the shots. Insisting on new methods and huge investment in new technology, they educated the enormous wine producers in La Mancha to make the sort of wines that would better appeal to you and me. So the lumbering big thunderbolts were banged on the head, and some fresh, aromatic wines were produced instead; from the same grapes, the white Airen and the red Cencibel (alias Tempranillo), from the same arid hot plains, but reborn in new wave style. To begin with these wines were sold anonymously behind branded wine labels, concealing their origins. But La Mancha is gaining its own respect now, and you'll find it increasingly on the label, perhaps not as the most prominent name – but underneath names such as Castillo de Alhambra.

Red   Reds from La Mancha are definitely worth a second look. Now the producers have got the hang of integrating new technology into their character-giving traditional methods, you get some rich, voluptuous fruit-jam wines, often rounded by oaky vanilla. Sometimes they may appear altogether too sweet and jammy, but how much better to have succulent sweet fruit than too much heavy-handed alcohol. They often represent the best value for money at the bottom of the price scale that you can find on the shelves.

White   The whites are less spectacular. Advanced technology has swept aside the coarse, sometimes downright unpleasant attributes of these hot-country whites, but has left a curiously unripe quality to them – almost like the sting of green nettles you get from English wines – overlaid with pear drops. Fuller, riper examples can be too soupy to be interesting. There are better cheap and cheerful whites around to choose.

Navarra

Having once engulfed Rioja as part of its kingdom, Navarra now lives in the shadow of its former underling, squashed between Rioja to the south and the Pyrenees to the north. But the shadow is being consciously shrugged off now, helped by one of the most advanced vine and vinification research stations in Spain. Garnacha, which makes a good line in rosés, incidentally, is the dominant red variety in Navarra, but there are now big incentives to plant either the Tempranilla (Rioja's top grape) or Cabernet Sauvignon instead. For white wines, Rioja's favourites again champion, with a recent authorisation having been passed to plant Chardonnay, too.

Red **A bit like junior Rioja, as you might expect (given its provenance) although with a snappy, highly accessible, individual style. There are some well-priced young reds on the shelves, with bouquets of just-squeezed grape juice touched by the faint aroma of rising dough. On the taste, the grape juice quality remains intact, though you realise it has lost the promised sugar (and just as well). An attractive zip of acidity puts it on its toes to make it a marvellously simple glugging 'any time' wine. I have come across older versions, too, dark as coffee and tasting not dissimilar; not nearly so likeable.**

White **The whites can also be rather old-fashioned, reeking of damp straw and tasting rather like you imagine it would. Roll on the influence of the research station!**

Penedès/Torres

The indomitable Catalan spirit thrust the Penedès region just south of Barcelona into the limelight not merely of Spanish wine production, but of world wine production. Traditionally, this area, although strongest in the white wine department, was designated by the Barcelona magnates as the kitchen garden for cheap red plonk. But realising the potential versatility of the terrain, cooled by a range of mountains sheltering it from the heat blowing in off the sea, the Catalans would have none of it. With the revolutionary wine company Torres at the forefront, they persevered with imported grape varieties coupled with the latest technology, to produce the most individualistic portfolio of wines created anywhere in Spain. Torres wines, sold more with the name Torres to the forefront than that of Penedès, are the most diverse – and the most widely available – offering the full gamut from deeply traditional to totally innovative.

There's really no such thing as a typical Penedès wine. Certainly there are classic Penedès grapes, but these may either be transformed by new methods, or (and watch out)

be martyrs to tradition, being allowed to become oxidised, flat and stale. At present the major taste of Penedès on the wine shop shelves is the taste of wines from the Torres bodega, so here are notes on the company's most widely available wines.

Viña Sol Made 100 per cent from the local white Parellada grape with all the might of new technology behind it, this is a clean, 'green' white wine with a piercing lemony bouquet tinged by a whiff of hyacinths. On the taste, there's a hint of Golden Delicious apples with their slight and fleeting taste. Representative of many 'new style' Penedès whites, this is a great aperitif wine.

Gran Viña Sol The Parellada gives up 30 per cent of its share here to the Chardonnay grape. And it shows amazingly, overlaying rich icing sugar scents and peachy flavours on the clean white taste.

Viña Esmeralda Bags of spice and a little sugar (it's 'medium' in style) are to be found in this pungent white Muscat/Gewürztraminer blend.

Tres Torres Sangredetoro Made from a blend of local varieties, this is a meat pie of a red wine, with the scents of pastry and meat mingling in a slightly hot 'cooked' way. There's a meaty tang to the taste, too, with a rich fruity sauce. Big stuff, this; open it well before you want to drink it, and partner it with substantial meaty food.

The *Gran Sangredetoro* version is older, oakier and altogether rather smoother.

Coronas The Tempranillo grape here performs brilliant things, giving the rich scent of crumbled digestive biscuits and the vibrant, juicy-fruit flavours of a just-made redcurrant tart. A highly polished red wine, definitely in the dinner party class, when it would transform any roast or casserole with its sweet, fruity style.

Gran Coronas is the smarter version including 30 per cent classic Cabernet Sauvignon.

Ribera Del Duero

Slap in the middle of northern Spain, the little known wine-making enclave of Ribera del Duero is responsible for Spain's most expensive red wine – called Vega Sicilia – which is made from a local clone of the Tempranillo

blended with the Bordeaux classics. It certainly had
Winston Churchill fooled – he immediately confused it
with claret – and this confusion has surrounded other red
wines of the area, too, notably Pesquera.

Pesquera **This red is a rich, oaky treat with soft,
fruity scents and dry blackcurrant-skin flavours,
which has in its time been mistaken for the most
expensive Bordeaux going, Château Petrus.**

Rioja

Traditionally Spain's most highly prized quality wine
region, Rioja is certainly the flagship for Spain around the
world. A major and lasting boost to the area came in the
1860s, when the dreaded vine-attacking louse phylloxera
wiped out the vineyards of Bordeaux, and so drove the
experienced French wine-makers south over the
Pyrenees to find the as yet unravaged vineyards of Rioja.
New bodegas were built, and splendid wines heavily influ-
enced by Bordeaux techniques evolved. It took a good
century before these took the UK by storm, but by goodness were we pleased to see them in the early '70s? At last,
real class, real character, real velvet in the glass for ridicu-
lously little money.

Rioja wine-makers are masters of the jigsaw. With a
range of grape varieties (most importantly Tempranillo)
available to them, a variety of microclimates and a whole
list of options to choose from back in the bodega where the
wines are made and matured, they slot together the various components to make just the wine they want. One of
the secrets to what you are getting from any given bottle is
held on the back label. Sin Crianza denotes a very junior
wine, simple and easy drinking but quite untypical;
Crianza is the first step up the ageing ladder – rounder and
softer wines resulting. Reserva means the wine has been
aged in wood to add vanilla softness and longevity; while
Gran Reserva status is reserved for the best wines given
the full works, which includes two years ageing in oak
barrels and a further three in bottle. White Rioja can span
the breadth-of-flavour spectrum, too. The most usual style
is light and dry (and relatively characterless), while if you
get an example of the classic old sort, you'll find it dark
and broad and oaky . . . and seemingly almost past it
(though not quite).

Red **Because the wine-maker can piece together the jigsaw more or less how he likes, there is
a great variety of Rioja styles, ranging from**

springily young and liverish, through to solidly opulent and sedate. As the Rioja becomes more distinguished (see the scale of classifications on page 109), so it becomes more velvety and more intensely flavoured. But there are taste triggers common to all styles. The most obvious one is vanilla. Take a good sniff at a glass of decent Rioja and it puts you in mind of the best dessert trolley. Into the taste, and the vanilla persists, coating (appropriately) slightly stewed fruit. There's a lively acidity in there, too; in very young styles, this can seem a little too busy and unsettled, but in maturer versions it just sits up pertly at the end of the taste, rescuing the sumptuous pudding flavours from too much complacence. Although excellent mature Riojas used to be a real snip, sadly there are fewer of them around now, and certainly fewer bargains.

White White Riojas used to be expected to stand up to the wood-ageing dished out to the reds; and they didn't. The oak and the oxygen crushed the fruit and distorted the taste. Then along came new technology which altered the picture completely. Squeaky clean new style Riojas, led by Marqués de Cáceres, have a spiky fresh zing to them, tinged with the scent of pineapples and a slightly twiggy taste with the added zip of grapefruit. A very fashionable style for aperitif drinking, Rioja can also accompany delicate nouvelle cooking. There is also a new generation of oak-aged versions being born of 'new technology'; light years removed from their predecessors.

Rueda

The Rueda region north-east of Madrid has something the rest of Spain could well be envious of: a local white grape variety with bags of character. And for this reason, grand masters in the red wine business of Rioja and elsewhere have elected to concentrate their white wine efforts in Rueda instead of in their own home patch, installing the most expensive modern equipment going. The grape that has so concentrated the efforts of these giants of the wine world is the Verdejo, an entirely local variety which doesn't exactly make things easy for the vine grower, being an awkward type to grow successfully. But it has proved to be worth the effort, breathing new life into the region.

Rueda whites used all to be fortified to make them yet more alcoholic, but moving with the times, a thoroughly natural, crisp white style has emerged with fresh green leaf aromas and a slim fruitiness trimmed with intense chopped nut flavours. Traditionally, oak-ageing played a part in the process, and some wines are still made with a kiss of oak contributing more colour, body and a full custardy edge. Sauvignon Blanc has also been introduced into the region, bringing with it that sharp prick of acidity and the scent and taste of newly picked gooseberries.

Terra Alta

West of Tarragona (and south-west of Barcelona), this hilly inhospitable place has as little rain as anywhere in Spain, and makes the vines work hard to survive.

Whites are the thing here, packing an unusual tobacco note into the wine. Strongly coloured and strongly flavoured, there are powerful scents of the timber yard, softening to honey on the taste. Although dry, these wines are far from slim, and have plenty to chew on and a faint sting in the mouth – to continue the analogy, as you might expect from chewing tobacco.

Toro

Although the Toro region (named after the highly revered bull), just to the west of Rueda, has been making wine for longer than most parts of Spain, it was only officially demarcated in 1987.

Red wines are the thing here, made from the big, tannic Tinto de Toro grape. And are they beefy? It's dense, dark, strapping stuff, red Toro, highly alcoholic and with solid meaty flavours and a curious, slightly eggy end note. Certainly it needs opening an hour or two before being served, and then must be partnered by an equally muscular meal with red meat as the main course.

Valdepeñas

The Valdepeñasites were so confident of the superior quality of their wines, made in an enclave to the south of the great La Mancha plain, that they fought for their own Denominación de Origen – and got it. As in La Mancha, the white Airen grape is by far the most widely planted, but it is for her red wines (based on the Cencibel, alias Tempranillo) that Valdepeñas is justifiably famed. Traditionally, wines were made exclusively in enormous Ali Baba clay jars, not exactly designed to preserve the squeaky clean freshness that is so highly prized by today's wine lovers. So now giant stainless steel silos, often standing like fairy tale castles outside in the sun, have to an extent taken over from the picturesque pots, and marvellously soft, gluggable wines are the consequence.

Red   Where reds are concerned, a successful recipe is for them to be made in stainless steel, then stored first in the Ali Baba jars, before being transferred to oak barrels to finish off the maturation. And they are still sold, even at seven or eight years old, at very reasonable prices. Despite their maturity, these are perennially youthful wines with thrusting berry scents mingling with the buttery smell of raw cake mixture on the bouquet, leading you into the delicious flavours of loganberries and cherries coated with vanilla custard on the taste. Although at the price, you might consider knocking a bottle back with plates of spaghetti, good Valdepeñas reds are certainly up to a smart dinner party, when they'll partner red meat and cheese most successfully.

White   The whites are rather more disappointing. The essential new technology introduced to streamline the ragged, often off, scents and flavours have in some instances cleaned up the act so thoroughly that there's precious little left bar the feeling the wine is meaner and slighter than was intended.

Valencia

Early in the seventeenth century, Valencia wines were classified as 'supreme, intermediate or ordinary' – and still today qualitative judgements of Valencia wines revolve more around how good they are than *how* they are; they can be all things to all men. Supermarket and wine chain wine buyers visit the Valencia region inland from the active port of the same name, with a specification in their hands of what precisely they want, and the big bodegas do their best to fill it. Whereas the brewery chains used to buy their bulk-buy wines from La Mancha to stick inside anonymous branded bottles, now Valencia is the place instead.

Picturing
the
Taste

Riesling

petrol
nettles
revving-up aeroplane
honey
sap in a snapped twig
lime
green apple

Sauvignon Blanc

gooseberries
cat
cut grass
asparagus
green apples
green leaves
grapefruit

Sémillon
butter
egg custard
straw
toast
mangoes
apricots
candle wax

Gamay
iodine
gymshoes
tar
cherries
jam
raspberries
fruit kernel

Pinot Blanc

cream
apple
citron pressé
lavender
Parma violets
canned lychees
bracken

Nebbiolo

truffles
prunes
violets
liquorice
chocolate

Chardonnay

butter
peach
honeysuckle
French pâtisserie
clover
pineapple
angelica

Merlot

velvet
red berry fruits
plums on the branch
Dundee cake
toffees
pencil sharings
mint

Syrah

raspberries
fruit gums
pepper
creosote
leather and saddle soap
goulash
biscuits on baking sheet
a naked foot

Chenin Blanc

grapefruit
damp straw
honey
wet wool
cheese
kiwi fruit
concentrated orange juice
sprinkling of sugar

Pinot Noir

strawberries
cabbages
gamey meat
cherries
rusty metal
earth
compost

Gewürztraminer

scented soap
exotic fruits
China tea
pot pourri
cinnamon type spices

Cabernet Sauvignon

blackcurrants
violets
cigar box
rosehip
green capsicum
cake
brick

Cabernet Franc

raspberries & blackcurrants
sponge cake & crumbs
grass & green leaves
herbaceous border
sharp steel knife

But gone is the anonymity now: the replacements are definitely Valencia wines – and cheaper than the brands were, too. They come in all colours and styles, with a range of bottle sizes (the giants aimed at the party market) to come.

Red The red can be bright and zingy and highly drinkable (good value for money, hooray!). The bouquet has a slightly hot, cooked – almost toffeeish – aroma, leading you into soft fruit cake flavours with flavours of dried fruits and cherries. It makes an excellent party wine, is good for drinking on its own or with simple food.

White The dry white is water white and not much more positive on the bouquet, although the faint scent of lemon can be found if you look hard enough. A slight wine, you could say, nothing much to thrill – though not much to offend either. A slight sweetness is detectable, knocked back by pleasant acidity. It must be very young and very cold, and then it's fine for occasions when it won't exactly be the focal point. The medium version is the same only sweeter – and rather more cloying, so needs to be served colder still.

Portugal

 PORTUGAL IS UP THERE with the big boys in wine-producing terms; only six countries in the world produce more wine than she does. But you'd never guess it, would you? Britain's oldest ally is best known for port and Mateus Rosé, which gives a very restricted view of this huge, diverse and potentially exciting wine country.

The trouble has always been introspection and, I suppose, a measure of complacency. You see, traditional Portuguese wines simply didn't travel. That's what traditional Portuguese wine producers thought and we obediently believed them. I don't mean they became sick on the way, or ended up on our dining tables tasting any different from the way they were when they set out, it's just that they would never have tasted appealing to the British palate in the first place. So to launch them on a journey to our waiting wine shelves didn't make much sense, and the Portuguese saw little point in trying to temper the style of her wines to suit foreign palates; they went down well enough at home as they were.

Old-fashioned Portuguese wines were just that, old-fashioned. When modern vinification techniques were adopted around the world for making wines more accessible, softer and more instantly likeable, Portuguese wines, being vinified by clumsy, outdated methods, remained forbiddingly brutish and tough. It must be admitted that the Portuguese themselves, having little experience of squeaky clean new wave wines made elsewhere (they made plenty of their own to satisfy domestic appetites, so why bother to experiment?), were quite happy with their old-fashioned thunderbolts. But it ceased to make sense remaining quite so insular once they became part of a Common Europe in 1986 and so, with assistance from grants and subsidies paid to improve quality, new ideas, new technology and new-tasting wines gradually began to be introduced.

As a natural resource, Portugal has a rich abundance of unusual native grapes. Where the rest of the world has clamoured to plant the buzz international varieties such as Chardonnay, Cabernet Sauvignon, Sauvignon Blanc *et al*, Portugal has largely remained faithful to her own individual fruit, and what a good thing, too! There is something rather repetitive about the game of international copy-cat played by the highly competitive high rollers. There are, after all, about a thousand different wine-making grape varieties to choose from, and it's refreshing to have a crack at some of the other nine hundred and eighty less usual types, rather than simply continuing to taste different variations on the theme of the most fashionable few.

Red wines have historically always been Portugal's forte – she actually makes four times more red wine than white. As well as her traditional old favourites such as Dão, always heralded as the flagship (though more a thundering old oil tanker than stream-lined ocean liner in the past), there is a variety of other updated traditionals coming on stream, as well as some terrific innovations, sometimes using classic grape varieties, sometimes the indigenous types and sometimes a mixture of the two. Whites are dominated by Vinho Verde – a wine that has found itself naturally in fash-ion – and there are others worth looking out for, both traditional style and new.

Although the only official classification system for Portuguese wines revolves around demarcated areas such as Dão, Bairrada and Douro (each of which is a wine-producing region), Portuguese wine producers are not nearly so hung up on places as are the French, or on grape varieties, as are producers in the new world. They are freer spirits, really, inspired wine-makers being able to come up with winning wines and being able to market them simply on the strength of their name. Individual names have always been very important in Portuguese wine circles. There is no quality hier-archy to get to grips with – and few added twists to the wording on the label which will enlighten you about the style or quality of the wine inside the bottle, so the names of well known and respected wine producers appearing on the label of a bottle have, in a way, provided their own 'guarantee' of quality.

Among the few terms classifying a wine's style, you may find *Garrafeira*, which indicates that a red wine has matured for at least three years, with a minimum of one in bottle. Some wines call themselves simply Garrafeira, without indicating where the wine comes from; then you have only the name of the producer to go on. Maturing the wine for an adequate length of time, though, has historically never been a problem in Portugal; remember the taste was for big, old wines. When Portuguese wines (other than the ubiquitous Mateus Rosé, that is) first began to seep into British wine shops, there were some veritable old methusalas among them – too old for our tastes, but offered at temptingly bargain prices. Now they have rejuvenated a bit, but it is still possible to find regular Portuguese wines with no handles to boast that have clocked up as many years as the Garrafeiras. Prices, too, sadly have become more realistic. The wines' lives have been shortened and their prices lengthened by rampant infla-tion at home.

So following this irregular pattern of nomenclature, Portugal's wines will be listed here idiosyncratically as they are: some by region and others by the name of the maker or brand. Most Portuguese wine is made by co-operatives and marketed by big companies giving their name to the wine. So 'brands' (generally a dirty word in lan-guages other than Portuguese) are nothing new to Portugal, and certainly nothing to be ashamed of. The bright new boys in the business making their new masters have been able simply to call them after the company name, and to slip into the market with the greatest of ease.

The Wines and Their Taste:

Arruda

Arruda (meaning rather unromantically 'road' as in Arruda dos Vinhos 'of the wines') is a small, pastoral town giving its name to the surrounding wine area north of Lisbon in Portugal's largest wine-producing region (as yet not officially designated). No-one would have known anything of it abroad had it not been for the British supermarket chain Sainsbury's, who gave the major co-operative there – responsible for a third of all Arruda wines – quite a shake-up. Give us good, juicy, fruity red wine and we'll sell all we can get, was the message. And they did; and Sainsbury's have. The grape varieties used won't mean much to you (they don't to me), but they certainly do their stuff.

Red wines are almost invariably dry, and this is no exception, except that the fruit is so sweet, there's a succulent sweetness involved in the taste as well. It's like eating an orange with the peel on; a whole kumquat, which you tackle skin and all, combining the juicy fruitiness with the tart zest. There's a fleeting hint of orange blossom talc, too, an intense floweriness which leads you on into the surprisingly bitter, beefier tastes at the finish when you swallow.

Bairrada

This is another light Portugal has successfully been hiding beneath her bushel; highly rated at home, until ten years ago, much of the fine wine was bagged by big companies and sold under their own name as an anonymously sourced Garrafeira or Reserva. But the Bairrada region south of Oporto and west of the Dão area has officially been recognised now, and all Bairradas are sold as such. Reds dominate again, and are made largely from the Baga grape, renowned for making astringent, tannic wines that age well – and lengthily. New methods are being practised now to bring the wines on sooner, though; sooner than the decade or so they have historically been kept before drinking.

Red **A piercing bouquet is the first impression you get from these wines, vibrant and almost sharp. Look further and you may sense warm dough, and the attractive vanilla scent of crème anglaise. The less fruity versions may offer slightly heavy, earthy,**

almost muddy aromas at first whiff, perhaps the merest suggestion of camphor. Curiously, the flavour appears to be fragmented, with two distinct elements. There is an abrasive core of astringence and lively acidity bringing iron filings to mind, but also, quite separately, fruit – hooray – in the guise of damsons steeped in alcohol. The vibrant acidity definitely marks this as a 'with food' wine; good substantial meat pies and tarts being among the best partners.

White Can remind you of chrysanthemums on the bouquet, developing into good honest 'dry whites', sometimes with a hint of oaky vanilla to them.

Dão

This was the trail-blazer of the thunderbolts, the first unmodified Portuguese wine to get recognition in Britain. The River Dão gives its name to the rugged, mountainous region inland from Bairrada, freezing cold in winter and scorching from early summer through to the vintage at the end of September. The cocktail of local grapes used for reds are fermented skins and all, so expect deep colour and concentrated tannin from these wines which must, by law, be matured for a minimum (and it usually is a minimum) of eighteen months in oak casks. Twenty per cent of production is white wine, which also has to do time in oak casks – six months minimum, this time, giving a golden tone to the wine.

Red There is a bigger discrepancy in quality and flavour of both red and white Dãos than in any other classic wine I know. They range from the unspeakable through the unusual to the unusually delicious . . . the poor red examples are heavy, tough and lugubrious with hint of neither life nor fruit, while the white shockers are coarse and oxidised. But these are a dying style. Instead, on the nose of a good red Dão, you usually find a hint of iron, like the whiff of health spa water with a high iron content, and a slight touch of blood (you know how blood seems irony in smell?). From the nose, you might expect the taste to be tough, but you'll be surprised by the velvety softness of this wine, as though time has smoothed out all the harsh edges. The fruit content is a late runner in the taste medley, finishing it all off with the lingering after-taste of tangy wine berries (like sharper, shiny raspberries, if you haven't come across them). There's a vibrance to the taste, a slight sensation of acidity, and the subdued tannins leave the tongue feeling dry. Definitely food wine, Portuguese reds were not made to be sipped as aperitifs.

White New methods are bringing attractive lemony tones to the whites, which have two strong memory triggers: those of honey and of resin, contributing good strong character and individuality.

Douro

The scenic Douro river, slicing east to west through northern Portugal and gushing into the sea at Oporto, has historically lent its often precipitously steep valley sides to the cultivation of vines to make port. The port producing vineyards are far upstream in as remote and rugged a place as you will find in Europe, suffering the very extremes of temperate temperatures. All port-makers have used some of their grapes to make their own table wine, often fermenting them in furious heat in open concrete *lagares*. But recently the Douro has been demarcated as a table wine producer as well, and essential modern equipment, including temperature control for the fermentation tanks, has improved drinkability no end.

Grapes used for making table wines in the Douro are the same as for port, numerous hardy varieties which can withstand the winter's chill and summer's bake. And the tendency is for these grapes to make fairly mighty wines; the reds, certainly, needing to be opened a couple of hours before they will be served. There can be a suggestion of tar on the nose of these rusty-coloured, tannic heavyweights, and a bit of a thud to the taste, slightly clumsy fruitiness overlaid with the flavour of saturated wood. White Douros tend to be fresher and lighter on their feet.

João Pires

Setubal, south of Lisbon, is also home to the João Pires wine firm with its pioneering Australian wine-maker who has really put the name on the map with a number of highly individual brands. The flavour here is distinctly international, with classic grape varieties skilfully being integrated into the best local traditions.

Dry Moscato This is a very pretty, dry white wine, deliciously made from the aromatic, intensely 'grapey' Muscat grapes. The scents and flavours are as richly varied as a plate of petit fours sweets and biscuits – walnuts dipped in icing sugar, Cape gooseberries coated in icing – there's a rich and complex bouquet to this wine which concentrates into the lush taste of raisins when you have a sip, but dry. Marvellously interesting as an aperitif, well chilled, or with spicy savoury dishes such as stir-fries.

Tinto de Anfora A rich, fruity red wine which hints at toffee and old whisky casks on the nose, luring you into a dry toffeeish taste, if you can imagine it, which reminds you of burnt sugar.

Other wines from the same stable include the lovely fat, fruity winter red, **Meia Pipa** and the forward claret-like **Quinta da Bacalhoa**, plus, on the white side, **Catarina** made from three Portuguese grape varieties being the wine-maker, Peter Bright's full oaky answer to new world Chardonnay.

José Maria da Fonseca

This hundred and fifty year old wine firm, based in the Setubal peninsula south of Lisbon, has built up such a reputation for itself that it wines are named not after the demarcated areas in which they are made, but as brands flying the firm's banner. In general they tend to be local wines made good . . . they use traditional grape varieties in the main, and often make the wines following traditional methods, but with modern twists which lift them above their peers.

Periquita The Periquita farm belonging to the founder of José Maria da Fonseca gave its name to a grape of the same name, now widely planted in southern Portugal. Not surprisingly, there is a Fonseca wine of the same name, and a mighty chap it is, too. On the bouquet, there is a faint resemblance to plasticine held in your hot little mitt, a kind of bakelite, plasticky smell. But there's a zing to it, and a waft of fruit, too. On the taste, you find a strange meatiness and an evident toughness, but don't worry, nestling in the middle there's a positive suggestion of raspberries (tart ones with no sugar; this is very dry red wine) to delight in before the taste tails off leaving you with an unexpected egginess. In common with all Portuguese reds, this one doesn't respond well to having the cork whipped out, being instantly poured and served without grub. You need to give this wine time to soften – a couple of hours open before you pour, or leave the wine in the glass a while before taking your first sip. And you need to match it with food. It's a red meat wine, make no mistake, and will stand up well to savoury dishes (not fruity ones) in that line.

Other J. M. Fonseca wines to look out for, all red, are the highly traditional, strong, **Tinto Velho** the well-priced, curiously spiritous **Casa Portuguesa** with good vanilla and fruit flavours, and an excellent, deep, fruity **Garrafeira**.

Mateus Rosé

Mateus Rosé seems to have been specially designed for the indecisive British wine drinker. Neither red nor white, sweet nor dry, still nor sparkling, it is all things to all people, and soared to fame in the fifties before the super-market wine boom a couple of decades later. In its time, it has been the best selling wine in the world, although its popularity has slipped a bit now that we are surrounded by so much choice. But still, Portuguese rosés account for a quarter of all exports. You'll see the Sogrape name on the label, another of the mighty wine firms to have established a good name for themselves.

Resembling the inside of a conch shell in colour, the *pétillant*, or faintly fizzy, Mateus in its flagon bottle picturing a much spired castle, is a very pretty drink. Give it the tasting routine and you are reminded of a just-opened biscuit tin on the nose, and of red car sweets (the sort coated in icing sugar) on the palate. It has a hint of lemon sherbet to it, too. Must be very well chilled, when it makes a good alfresco drink – put ice cubes in if you like, it won't object – and a perfect picnic wine.

Vinho Verde

The white version has been a great success story for Portugal. Although more red 'green wine' is produced than white, it is the white that has travelled most successfully; 25 per cent of Portuguese wine coming to Britain is fashionably 'green'. The name actually has nothing to do with the appearance of the wine, as you might guess from this, but refers to the fact that it is drunk young – as young as possible. Innumerable different grape varieties are planted higgledy-piggledy in the large Vinho Verde area in the very north of the country, often trained to climb high into the trees. And, except for the cream of the wines, they are vinified together to make the generally medium dry, high in acidity, low in alcohol, slightly sparkling wines.

The cheapest Vinho Verdes, generally made by co-operatives in the area, can be over-sulphured and slightly musty and dirty tasting, so are best avoided. Good examples (generally from one of the big wine firms) make delicious summer drinking, though, with their lily-like scent and slightly sweet, highly scented taste – like sipping home-made rose water. There is a nice citrus acidity to them, too, softened by the sweetness. In dry versions, this can seem a bit too searing for its own good. Come a hot day in summer, a bottle pulled straight from the fridge is mouth-wateringly fresh as a glass in the sun, or excellent for buffets and parties, teaming well with chicken and light meats – and mixing well with a wide cross-section of guests.

Vino Verde	Bairrada
Douro	Arruda
Dão	José Maria de Fonseca & João Pires

Greece

 MUCH SONG AND DANCE was made in the classic writings of Ancient Greece about the country's wines. This incredibly early civilisation had the techniques for growing good grapes and making apparently splendid wine. And they passed much of their knowledge on to the Romans who, in turn, spread the word throughout Western Europe. But whereas the rest of Western Europe took the original seed of an idea and developed it this way and that to come up with the thousands of vinous miracles we find in our wine shops today, the Greeks appear to have been happy to stick with the prototype.

Certainly there are individual wines produced all over Greece's mainland and her islands, and sure, they have quite a range of flavours to boast to their names. But there is an overriding coarseness and clumsiness common to the vast majority. And that coarseness is born of unsubtle wine-making techniques that simply allow the wines to become oxidised. But don't get me wrong, it's not entirely an accident that they are like that. Oxidised wines are very popular in Greece, not merely with the locals, but with the visitors as well, myself included. Perhaps I've had too many marvellous meals on memorable Greek holidays, but I positively *like* the clumsiness and oxidation. But even so, Greek wines don't travel that well – they are essentially taverna wines, and unless they end up in a taverna at the end of their travels, or at least teamed with taverna food, they founder at the dinner table.

It is commonly believed that all Greek wines are resinous. They are not. Only Retsina has that curious piney scent and flavour, and while other Greek wines often have broad, unusual character, these are not to be confused with the powerful individuality of Retsina.

The Wines and Their Tastes:

Demestica

Although this sounds like (and seems like) the generic name for Greek table wine, it's actually the brand name of a single wine made by the big producer Achaia-Clauss.

Red The red, though very washed out in appearance, in fact packs quite a punch of flavour, with the sweet blackberry scent of concentrated syrup. There's a refreshing acidity on the palate and yet more piercing berry flavours. The high acidity again sets it up well with rich and oily food.

White The white trails a bit on the likeability stakes, having a bit too much of the nail polish factory about it. There's a herbiness behind the acetone, though, like gentle marjoram, and a sweetness you don't entirely expect. But for all that, it definitely doesn't give the appearance (as do some too-pure-for-their-own-good wines) of having been sanitised for your protection, and is all the more characterful for it.

Wine-growing areas

Retsina

First, I'll explain why pine resin is added to these white wines – a somewhat unusual additive for any wine, you'll agree. Early Greeks stored their wines in clay jars with ill-fitting stoppers. Not surprisingly, the air got to the wine and quickly spoilt it. So a paste including pine resin was used to seal the cracks. This paste not only improved the keeping quality of the wine considerably, but also contributed its own character to it. Pine resin then became associated with better kept and better tasting wine, so the practice of actually adding it to the wine was introduced, and in Retsinas has continued to this day. The base wine may come from anywhere in Greece – and its origins become somewhat irrelevant, since they will certainly be blasted out by the added ingredient.

The fierce piney scent – almost like the pine part of a disinfectant – wafts out of a glass of Retsina with as much penetration as the menthol off a spoon of cough mixture. Into the taste, and the dominant element is the resin, giving a strange taste like the smell of camphor. There's an unusually harsh character to this wine, a keen rapier edge that will slice through even the greasiest food with nimble agility. The perfect partner, of course, is Greek food, and its uncanny ability to go with dolmades, moussaka, kebabs, Greek salad, the lot, makes me think it must have a much wider matching potential than we think.

Austria

AUSTRIA NEVER exported vast volumes of wine to Britain, but there was a certain affinity between her wines and our tastes. That is up until 1985. It seems cruel to harp back to the murky past, but the scandal principally involving Austrian wines (although there were German and Italian culprits as well) wiped them clean off the shelves and out of our lives for a good five years.

You'll remember, perhaps, that during the scandal certain wines were proved to have been adulterated with diethylene glycol, a by-product of antifreeze. The reason for adding it was to aid an illicit sweetening process. You see, most Austrian wines are essentially dry in style, but their largest export market, Germany, had more use for sweet wines. So Austria did her best to oblige – albeit illicitly, and rather dangerously. Only certain producers were involved, but nevertheless the reputation of all Austrian wines slumped to an all-time low, and only now are we beginning to see them creeping back on to our shelves again.

Trying desperately to disassociate themselves from Germany and to carve out their own new niche, a number have come back with a changed identity. The new style Austrian wines have jazzy modern labels now, with no semblance of gothic script, and are presented either in Burgundy-shaped bottles, or Bordeaux ones with shoulders. And every single one, be it a traditional German look-alike or one of the new style, wears a red and white 'Banderol', either around the capsule, like a scarf, or over the top of it. This is to signify that every minute detail of the wine and its heritage has been checked according to what Austria claim to be the strictest wine laws in the world.

Although Austria is trying to be very un-German now, there's no getting away from the fact that there are parallels. There is cross referencing in grape varieties, and in the quality scale used (Tafelwein, Qualitätswein, Spätlese, Auslese, etc.), although in general the wines we are seeing are dry – bar one or two sticky sweeties. There is also a smattering of 'international' grape varieties seen on the labels too – white grape varieties, that is (Austria concentrates more on whites than reds), such as Chardonnay and Pinot Blanc. Most distinctive among the reds is St-Laurent, Austria's own red grape variety, which makes a lively, richly blackcurranty wine bursting with sweet, juicy fruit. Her own idiosyncratic white grape variety is Grüner Veltliner, which is spearheading Austria's re-entry into the export market.

The Main Grape and its Taste:

Grüner Veltliner

Never has a grape variety been more onomato-poeic! When the new vintage is just released, it tastes exactly how its name suggests. Brand new Grüner Veltliner is green, vibrant and piquant with a leafy green taste. It can be almost too raw for its own good at first, it's better to wait until mid sum-mer before tackling the new batch. Then it settles down, and you can find a soft spiciness peering through the greenery. There can be creamy vanilla flavours touched by the – again green – scent of spinach water, and on the finish the merest touch of pepper.

Wine-growing areas

England

ENGLISH WINE, that is wine made from wine-making grapes grown outside in England or Wales, is no joke. And nor is it simply a rich man's folly. It is serious business for those people involved and fully justifies their commitment.

Contrary to popular belief, England does – in a good year, that is – have the climate for growing the right grapes. They don't actually need constant blasts of unbearably hot sun to become sufficiently ripe to make good wine. In fact, for them to have to struggle a bit during the growing season is no bad thing, although it must be admitted that if the weather is too unkind, no wine – or at least no decent wine – can be made.

Sharing roughly the same latitude with Germany's best wine regions, English conditions are not that dissimilar to theirs, and I believe England has the potential for making great wine, especially white. Perhaps it is either because of the damper, more temperamental climate, or because the English have wetter, less determined spirits, that a serious wine industry has never been established in England before. But wine-making grapes have been grown in Britain since Roman times, although the modern English wine craze goes back only three decades.

There are about 400 serious wine-makers in Britain, all producing wine on a small scale compared to some of the massive operations in Continental Europe. So all English wine production is hand-crafted, there are no giant vinification plants and it is all, therefore, in effect château bottled (which accounts for the fact that there is no such thing as a bargain price among English wines).

When the new enthusiasts planned their vineyards in the sixties and seventies, many naturally took their lead from Germany, planted German grape varieties and used German wine-making methods. But others branched out and either planted French varieties, or vinified traditional and new German grapes in French style. So there are two distinct types of English wine: those of the German school with a bit of residual sweetness, and the bone dry French. Information about whether the wine is dry, medium dry or sweet is likely to be expressed on the label. But whatever grapes and whichever method favoured, it is astonishing that a very definite English wine taste has emerged. English wines are distinct from all others, not because they are extraordinary or in some way freaks, but because they simply have their own individual English character.

The most widely planted grape variety is Germany's most prevalent, the Müller-Thurgau, with the Schonburger, Reichensteiner, Gutenborner etc. being frequently seen as well. Courageous attempts are being made with the Pinot Noir batting for the reds and so far, early attempts are looking pretty rosy. Where an individual grape variety dominates in the bottle, it is likely to be declared on the label, although there are also anonymous blends made from a hotchpotch of grapes.

A large variety of English wines is seen on the wine shop shelves, although not all at the same time. Because production is on a small scale, individual shops and small chains of shops tend each to have their own representatives, simply because insufficient volume is made to push a single wine round an enormous number of outlets. So the wine you buy will probably be equivalent to an individual one-off. I will therefore write a general taste note of the triggers that make a wine peculiarly English in taste.

But before I do, one word of warning. Do make sure you buy *English* wine, not British. There is a very big difference. Legally, an English wine has to be made from grapes grown in England or Wales, whereas a British wine – and the distinction is historic – is a wine made in the country from grape concentrate imported from abroad and reconstituted with tap water before being made into thoroughly sub-standard so-called wine. It used to benefit from a tax advantage and so be comparatively cheap, but now that that has been taken away, there is no point at all in buying it.

The Taste:

English Wine

Imagine a bed of young nettles and the smell they release when you tread on them (with your shoes on, I hope); there you have the most characteristic scent of English wines. There's a hint of bracken shoots to them, too, and, if you can recall it, the kind of herbaceous scent of unscented flowers – that's in there as well.

▨ *Wine-growing areas*

Lebanon

ODDITIES AMONG WINES tend to be more interesting on paper than they are in the glass. There is a remarkable exception, though, and that is Château Musar, made in the Lebanon. In the thick of the Bekaa Valley, with the front line of the war cutting between the vineyards and the winery, a brilliant wine-maker trained in Bordeaux called Serge Hochar manages to make a wine that is as delicious and well priced as it is exceptional. It is based on Cabernet Sauvignon with the southern French grapes of Cinsaut and Syrah.

The Best-known Wine:

Château Musar

Wet leather, gravy and rhododendron flowers mingle to make up the bouquet of this full-charactered red wine. When you taste it, you find ripe cherry fruit jostling with vanilla and a tang of spice. The sweetness of the fruit combined with the soft spiciness calls to mind spicy fruit pie with a lingering sensation of cinnamon and cloves. Then there's the characteristic pepperiness of the southern French grapes to finish. This is a marvellous dinner party wine, providing an excellent foil for red meat dishes, with offal being a key partner and, surprisingly, turkey.

Major wine-growing area

Eastern Europe

Introduction

THERE IS NOWHERE better than Eastern Europe to illustrate the extraordinary British wine-buying revolution that has taken place over the last twenty years. Being principally a beer drinking country, we were pretty immune to the various vinous delights of the world up until the early seventies. And we were rather shy about making choices as well, and so were very grateful to be able to buy wine, rather like soap powder, by well-known brands. From the Eastern Bloc we could comfort ourselves with the cosy well-known names of Bull's Blood from Hungary (well not exactly cosy, maybe, but well-known anyway) and Laski Rizling from Yugoslavia. Those who felt a bit more confident sought out – again, well-known – château wines from France and individual estate wines from Germany, but they had to dip quite deeply into their pockets for those.

What was really needed was something more individual than the ubiquitous brands ... and more accessible than France's châteaux-bottled clarets: individual wines in a range of familiar styles, with simple labels at affordable prices. And up stepped Bulgaria. At last here was Cabernet Sauvignon, the main claret grape variety, at a fraction of the price, and then Chardonnay, and once we had grown confident with those, other more unusual types followed. But we were ready for them. Eastern Europe had caused a revolution on our wine shelves and we have never been the same (thank goodness) since.

Bulgaria's immaculately timed and precisely targeted thrust into the British market was followed, rather less confidently, it must be said, by various sallies by her neighbouring countries, who bravely stepped out of the branded mould to bring us a mixed bag of new things: some very good, others that need a bit more work on them. The latest contenders in the market are various states from the Soviet Union, very green to the export game as yet, but old hands at making good individual wines.

Bulgaria

IT WASN'T EXACTLY by design that Bulgaria had so organised her vineyard operation at home that she could take on the world to become the second largest exporter of bottled wine. Coincidence had quite a big role to play. Building up to the revolution of 1944, Bulgaria had the shakiest rural economy in Europe. Peasant farmers were so poor, many pulled the wooden ploughs to till the soil themselves; they couldn't afford animals to do it instead. But then the whole agricultural policy was turned on its head, smallholders were organised into large, viable co-operatives, and along came mechanisation.

Until the advent of high tech machinery, grape varieties grown were obscure indigenous types (Bulgaria had been at this wine-making lark for longer than most, claiming a vinous history spanning up to six thousand years). And these local varieties trailed in a disorderly fashion close to the ground where they were well protected from the winter cold. This was not a convenient way for a vine to conduct itself where mechanical harvesters and the like were concerned, however. High tech equipment requires grapes to be organised to grow accessibly on the edge of shoulder-tall bushes, and that wasn't at all acceptable to these local types. So there was nothing for it in the fifties but to import more obliging varieties from Western Europe to supplant Bulgaria's indigenous strains; varieties such as Cabernet Sauvignon, Merlot, Chardonnay, Riesling, Ugni Blanc and a clone of the Muscat for the revamped, updated vineyards sited on the country's most favourable slopes.

By the time we Western wine drinkers were ready to be a shade more adventurous with our pennies in the early 1970s, these vineyards had had time to settle down, and the wine-makers had got to grips with every technical innovation available to them. Meanwhile the agricultural research stations had developed further obliging varieties such as Misket and Bulgarian Riesling, which you now also see in force on wine labels.

Apart from such incidental attributes as likeability and price, it is the labels themselves which have, in part, been responsible for Bulgaria's runaway success (only three countries sell more wine to Britain than she does), because they are dead simple to understand. Only the very cheapest blends (normally given a brand name) conceal the grape varieties concerned. Normally they are emblazoned across the label, which is complicated by little other information bar that of specifying the region from which the wine comes, and generally some indication of quality. Admittedly these regions may not mean much to you, and nor should you mind about that, because the differences between them are subtle, to say the least. But there are regions acclaimed for their brilliance at producing certain types of wine and I'll list these briefly.

As far as quality goes, although all wines are assessed and graded, there are only a few words you need to look out for to put each in its class. The dizzy top status is *Controliran*, meaning the wine comes from a defined region and is made from the right grapes in the right style to qualify. There are twenty *Controliran* wines in all, but only seven that you need consider at present, although more are on their way. For the record, these are Svischtov Cabernet Sauvignon, Oriachovitza Cabernet Sauvignon/Merlot, Suhindol Gamza, Asenovgrad Mavrud plus the new Lozitza Cabernet Sauvignon and Sakar Merlot batting for the reds, and Novi Pazar Chardonnay alone for the whites. Reds are definitely Bulgaria's forte.

Next down the scale you come to the *Reserve* wines, which have done time in wood – three years for reds and two for whites – with the new class of *Country Wines* being the equivalent of France's *Vin de Pays*. It may occur to you that 'Country Wine' isn't a particularly Bulgarian-sounding designation; because Britain provides such a whopping market for the stuff, this is an instance of the tail wagging the dog. The Great British public needed a 'country wine' class of well-priced, known variety wines . . . and so that is exactly what we got.

The Grapes and Wines and Their Taste:

Aligoté

Of all European grapes, this slightly mean and tart type from Burgundy seems an odd one to choose for Bulgaria's vineyards. And what does it produce there? Slightly mean, tart white wine, with a faint connotation of turpentine. The astringence strikes you at first sniff, when it attacks the inside of the nose, and continues on to the bitter end. There's a familiar nail polish remover scent in there, too, quite a feature of Bulgaria's inexpensive wines. I'd definitely help it along with a smidgen of fruit liqueur or syrup in the bottom of the glass, such as cassis, mûre or grenadine.

Cabernet Sauvignon

Trail-blazer of Bulgarian wines into Britain, the Cabernet Sauvignon has become a kind of cult, being equally attractive to connoisseurs who have been 'charmed by its presumption' as it is to bargain hunters and wine drinkers new to the game. There are now many grades of Cabernet Sauvignon available, the price climbing steadily with the quality.

Cheaper versions of this red wine are a bit tough and unfriendly, with strong evidence of harsh tea-leaf type tannins. The rush of blackcurrant fruit flavours you expect are deadened by heavy-handed wood and transient nail polish flavours. Climb up a rung or two and the fruit starts to dominate – although you'll still find an inky sourness that cries out for food (don't make the mistake of serving a junior 'BCS' as an aperitif or party wine). Up to the top echelons (the Svischtov Cabernet Sauvignon, for instance), and you're into the realms of enticing blackcurrant jam. The fruit cake bouquet leads you into a light-handed sweetness and succulence, ending on a positive, peppery note. Still wine for food, though (red meat, roasts and *mélanges*); like claret, this serious Cabernet Sauvignon wine is designed for the table.

Cabernet/Merlot Blend

The combination of these little sweeties together is a red winner; jammy, ripe fruit with the soft scent of blackcurrants. The taste has elements of a blackcurrant sandwich, if you can imagine such a thing; blackcurrants sandwiched between fresh slices of bread and butter.

Chardonnay

Bulgaria is struggling to keep up with the British thirst for Chardonnay, her production of this white wine being in very short supply. She's planting as much as she sensibly can (let's hope this diverse wine-producing country doesn't become another monotonous Chardonnay plantation), but against the odds. The last few harvests have produced very feeble yields, so the most basic quality has been withdrawn – simply to be channelled into the next class up.

In case the basic quality returns, let me tell you about it, though; mashed digestive biscuits on the nose with honey wrestling with nail polish remover on the taste. Stepping up, Khan Krum (which is a region) puts out a terrifically woody Reserve wine – first sniff transports you straight to a timber merchant's yard. Oak definitely dominates the taste, but in rather a likeable way, contributing its own smoky, bonfire flavour and pushing forward the sweet honeyed fruit. This is a natural companion

for smoked food – unless you want to get away from
bonfire flavours. The Special Reserve is altogether
subtler, pegging down the oak and adding spice
and almost a piney quality to the peachy fruit.

Mavrud

An inky-dark indigenous red grape, considered the pride
of Bulgaria on the home market. Look at a glass of this
stuff and you could be forgiven for wondering if it contains
black treacle; it's dense, dark and viscous.

There's a strange wet plastic mac connotation to
the bouquet (and never has a wet plastic mac smelt
so appealing, I might add) which leads you into the
meaty, chewy taste, dry and drying in the mouth but
spiked with rich, serious fruit. This is how *all* wines
used to be, and delicious we thought them, too. Now
it is unusual for its weight and density; winter wine,
definitely (unless you are in the habit of closeting
yourself before a fire with a plate of goulash on
your knee in high summer). Cut out for serving with
a hock of ham or a pot of stew; or a good match for
thick meaty main course soups.

Mehana

This is not actually the name of a grape, but a brand name
meaning 'tavern', attempting to convey a cheap-and-
cheerful bistro atmosphere. The medley of indigenous
grapes is altogether too complicated (and changeable) to
mention on the label, but all I can say is that it works well.

Red It has a welcoming sweet, cakey bouquet
and juicy fruit flavour, which is as good an introduction to red wine as you could possibly want.
However, since the British thirst for Bulgarian
wine is apparently taking an upward swing in the
quality stakes, Mehana is in danger of being
squeezed out.

White Nasturtiums and poppies are what the
bouquet of this grape-blend brand call to mind.
The wine appears at first encounter to be dry, but
wham, there you have it, an apparently superim-
posed layer of sweetness as well. Not as satisfactory
as the red equivalent, it must be said.

Melnik

This red grape has its roots planted firmly in Bulgaria's history, dating back to the first Bulgarian kingdom in 681.

On the bouquet, I can detect fleeting scents of oil cloths; like an oiled waterproof coat, or a flickering oil lamp with a new wick. And the taste carries this flavour trigger through pretty faithfully, introducing an attractive tarriness and the lovely sting of sweet cherries. The balance of flavours is a subtle one, well orchestrated and satisfying. A good, complete middleweight red wine.

Merlot

Like the Cabernets, Bulgarian Merlots vinified as single variety wines reward extravagance; the cheapies aren't quite as cheerful as you would hope.

In its most basic incarnation, this red grape presents you with rather a raw, indigestible bouquet, so the noticeably high acidity comes as little surprise on the palate, and strikes you well before the soft, slightly uneasy fruit has had the chance to impress. But splash out on something as special as the Stambolovo Special Reserve and you get a very different picture. The bouquet offers the ripe scent of plums *en branche*, fruit and wood bark rolled into one. The plummy fruit continues in overdrive on the taste, the fleshy flavour preventing the pencil-shaving wood tinge from getting above itself.

Merlot/Gamza Blend

The Gamza is a traditional Bulgarian red grape variety, and contributes leathery notes to the blend. The bouquet has that faint suggestion of the cheesy foot to it, pleasantly offset by soft, plummy fruit and ending with an attractively sweet finish.

Misket

The Misket is a funny little red grape used to make white wines – or, more frequently, parts of wines, since it is usually seen in blends. It contributes a grapeyness to wines lacking grapey characters, and there's not much more to say of it than that!

Muskat

A member of the familiar Muscat family, this white grape, although capable of making good grapey wine in its own right, is more often seen blending with something tart and sharp (such as Ugni Blanc), bringing attractive raisiny flavours to the bouquet and taste; Battenberg cake steeped in sherry, is one way of looking at it.

Riesling

In the past Bulgarian Riesling claimed to be none other than Rhine Riesling, although I must say, you could have fooled me . . . on the taste, it certainly seemed to have more in common with the Rizling (no relation) of Eastern Europe, but there you go. And suddenly, hey presto, the so-called Rhine Riesling disappeared – and none other than Welsch Riesling, as it should be called, took its place. Could it really be that the Rhine Riesling vines keeled over and were replaced by Welsch Riesling? The wines taste remarkably similar if that is the case.

There's definitely a soapiness to the bouquet, which is also remarkable for its lack of acidity. Into the flavour, and there's a faint spiciness, almost a resinous quality to this soupy white wine, totally lacking grip or bite. It's frequently used to blend with other varieties such as the Misket.

Sauvignon

Believing, as I do, that steely dry whites are far from being Bulgaria's strongest point, it's comforting to find a faint varietal character showing through in this wine.

The bouquet has tinges of grapefruit about it, and a slight flowery edge; unfortunately, though, good old nail polish remover hogs the limelight in the taste – and it must be said, gives it a bit of body in an oily sort of way. Dry and nondescript otherwise, with a lingering nondescript taste.

The Main Wine-producing Areas:

Essentially the country divides simply into four quarters, with the Balkan mountains sweeping through the middle, west to east. The top right quarter concentrates on white wines, top left and middle make elegant, refined styles, with the south containing some of the most highly rated areas for reds.

Top left, you have the so-called northern region, in general concentrating on red wines. Within this quarter you find the top-rated **Suhindol** complex of villages, vineyards and the renowned Suhindol winery. Cabernet Sauvignon is the dominant variety here – and the combination of Suhindol and Cabernet is generally a good one – although it is for the native Gamza grape that Suhindol earns *Controliran* status. **Svischtov** is up here, too, along with the newly introduced *Controliran* region of **Lozitza**. Russe, which you'll see on the label in connection with white varieties, is at the top right of the region on the border with Romania.

The major region for the classic white grape varieties on which Bulgaria feels obliged to concentrate now that the demand for dry white wine is so urgent, is the so-called eastern region, top (and centre) right. Here you have the important *Controliran* centre of **Novi Pazar** and equally famous **Khan Krum** (for it is a place, not a person) putting out Chardonnay like it is going out of fashion. **Burgas** and **Shumen**, natural habitats for less lustrous varietals, are also here.

South of the mountain range in the southern half, there is quite a concentration of names you will recognise from the label. In the south-western region, strong on red wines from classic grape varieties, you'll find **Melnik**, the name of a place as well as a grape variety.

Finally in the large southern region, red wines dominate again with **Oriachovitza** and **Sakar** being *Controliran* names to look out for, plus the highly regarded **Stambolovo** and **Asenovgrad**. **Plovdiv** is here too, an area putting out a range of qualities. To come are a handful of wines from **Sliven** (already sewing up the wine box demands) made from Cabernet Sauvignon and Pinot Noir, the area with the biggest potential for expansion. **Korten** is another name that will start to crop up, largely associated with cheaper Cabernet Sauvignons.

Northern	South-Western
Eastern	Southern

Hungary

UNTIL VERY RECENTLY, there has been something of a stagnation in Hungarian wines. The two old standard bearers, Bull's Blood and the stickily sweet Tokay, having waved the flag for their country for a good couple of decades, are still out there on their own waiting for support. It is coming slowly, trickling on to wine shop shelves here and there, but in such small volume and offering such enormously variable quality, that little impact has so far been felt.

These two stalwarts have quite a history attached to them. They carry a lot of weight at home and certainly had their devotees in Britain in substantial numbers, before the wine buying public of Great Britain gained enough confidence to strike out and shun the big brands. When we first started to buy lesser known idiosyncrasies from all over the world, there was a small attempt to include some of Hungary's other less well-known wines among the consignments coming from Budapest – and we were keen to have them. But not keen enough, it would appear, to assure their future. There has been much mismanagement in the marketing of Hungarian wines in the UK over the years, and with the agency for them being tossed like a shuttlecock from one importing agent to another, they lost their grip. It is only now with the opening up of the Eastern European market that we are again seeing what they can do outside the traditional centres of Tokay and Eger.

Various varietal wines made from grape varieties we all recognise (from the label, at least) are again beginning to filter in, but they've got quite a long way to go before they will represent any challenge to the Bulgars. Come across a Hungarian 'Chardonnay', say, in a blind tasting, and there's certainly no way of spotting what it actually is because it's not exactly overburdened with characteristic memory triggers. Of the classic varieties vinified in Hungary, the best two I have come across are Muscat and Merlot.

The Best-known Red Wine:

Bull's Blood

The story behind the somewhat peculiar name (Egri Bikaver in Hungarian, meaning Bull's Blood of Eger) is that back in the sixteenth century when the fortress of Eger was under attack from the Turks, the Magyars inside stood at the battlements downing tankards of the local wine to give themselves courage against a superior force. Seeing their apparently blood-stained beards, the enemy, believing the potion to be the blood of bulls, fled in terror.

and the siege ended painlessly. Based on local grape
varieties, in the past, Bull's Blood was a big, chunky wine,
as robust as they come, but gradually it has been lightened
over the years, supposedly to have greater commercial
appeal.

**Always boasting an old vintage on the label, the
purply hues of this wine look surprisingly youthful.
The bouquet has an attractive caramel quality with
a nice zing of fruit, cut by a rusty association,
almost a hint of the smell of blood. On the taste, the
fruit fades to almost nothing, giving way to tough,
firm tannins and an endorsement of the rustiness,
seeming so powerful now it is positively metallic –
like the taste of extremely cheap aluminium cut-
lery. Although a shadow of its former self, it's still a
big, dense, robust wine, this. Open well ahead of
time and plan to serve it with a substantial meal
of root vegetables, nut roast, hearty winter stew or,
of course, goulash, the most famous Hungarian
national dish.**

Yugoslavia

 YOU COULD BE FORGIVEN for considering Yugoslavia to be a one-grape producer.
One grape variety, that is, the Laski Rizling having traditionally represented
by far the strongest presence on British shelves. But with the fashion swing
away from wines sold by brand name on to individual grape varieties, she is
now beginning to show what other things she can do – and sometimes do very well.
Yugoslavia actually grows a wealth of different varieties, some local and obscure,
others members of the fashionable international set. As yet these have not caught our
imaginations as successfully as varietals from Bulgaria, but she's shown some promise, particularly with her delicate version of Cabernet Sauvignon.

The Best-known Wine:

Laski Rizling

It's only recently that the widely planted so-called Riesling of Eastern Europe has been obliged to call itself Rizling, to distinguish it from the noble variety of Germany to which it bears no resemblance at all.

This grape makes soupy white wine totally lacking in bite – and generally in character as well. Okay, so on the bouquet there is a slight hint of dahlias and michaelmas daisies – at the flower arranging stage, when you're tearing the leaves off to give that bitter sweet twang. But when you get to taste it you realise, on scrutiny by the buds, that it is actually rather harsh wine under an overlay of sweetness. It doesn't seem at all grapey, as you might expect; in fact, it can be difficult to imagine that it is a direct derivative of the grape at all. And it doesn't even get better once you've swallowed, because it leaves a sharp, rather acrid taste in the mouth for some time. If you still have plans to buy another bottle, make sure it is really cold when you serve it, and I would suggest matching it to a dish with a lot of garlic or other powerful flavourings to compensate for its shortcomings.

Wine-growing areas

North America

THE MODERN WINE industry in the United States of America is very 'new world'. That's not to say that the earliest settlers ignored vines and wine. Of course they didn't – there's hardly a settler to put his feet down on more or less temperate soil anywhere on the globe who didn't make wine something of a priority, and settlers to the various parts of America were no exception. Most of them relied on the indigenous species of grape, *vitis labrusca*, which flourished in various states, making curiously rank, musky, so-called 'foxy' tasting wine. California was, ironically, devoid of any indigenous vines, and the first varieties to be planted there were so-called Mission grapes, a primitive *vinifera* variety, brought by the Jesuits for sacramental purposes. In time, more European varieties were imported and planted side by side with the Mission and the native types and wine-making started to boom. But only briefly.

You'll remember that the Prohibition of alcohol went national in 1920 and reigned for a tyrannical thirteen years. Although great strides in wine-making had been made before that, there was no point in continuing to grow 'wine only' grapes any longer, so the majority of vineyards were grubbed up in favour of more versatile grapes that could produce fruit for eating and drying (as well as for concentrating into juice bricks which were sold in chemist shops, along with obliging sachets of yeast . . . and accompanying instructions not to mix the two: 'making wine is illegal' the instructions warned!). The brooding threat of serious competition to European wine producers was thus hobbled overnight. And even after the abolition of Prohibition, North America took a long time to spring back into form; it seemed for a while that the energy had left the business for good. The country was going through its worst depression and there was little inclination to invest in luxuries.

Those wine-makers restarting their businesses fell back on the native *labrusca* and dried fruit varieties, and old-fashioned – frequently fortified – wine styles. Such table wines as were being made were generally mass-produced, and despite their humble style, were sold under the assumed names of the European favourites such as Chablis and Burgundy. But gradually the classic *vinifera* grape varieties crept back in the forties, particularly in California, and the better wines began to be named after the (now thoroughly respectable) grape types from which they were made.

California continued to be the fulcrum of American wine. But the success it now enjoys with its wine was still a long way off. For the next couple of decades the large wine-making concerns yo-yoed between producing wine and being taken over by distillers to produce spirit. The children of the liberated sixties came to the rescue, though. Flower Power inspired individuals to 'do their own thing', and a fashionable 'thing' to do, was to go off and find your own plot to make your own wine. So the small 'boutique' wineries were started and injected a valuable new pride into wine-making. There are now about 690 wineries in California (as opposed to 200 odd in the early sixties), so you see what I mean about very new world.

Wine is made in the majority of the 50 states, with California being far and away the most important producer. Further north up the West Coast, Washington State makes sufficient volumes of wine to spare some for the British market, while the only other states you're likely to see represented – and then only in a tiny way – are the Eastern seaboard's New York and Texas, which have hit a few of the more recherché wine shelves with their wines in the last couple of years.

California

THE GOLDEN STATE, as it has been dubbed, is by far the most glittering wine producer in North America, responsible for producing 90 per cent of all her wines. It is home to the University of California at Davis, whose vital Department of Viticulture single-handedly converted wine-making from a haphazard art into a science. *Everything* has been analysed in precise scientific detail. Where, in Europe, the perfect sites for vineyards evolved over centuries of highly labour intensive trial and error, the land available in California has been scrutinised and analysed and squeezed into a highly precise pigeon hole. There's not an aspect that remains a mystery to prospective planters.

One of the most variable things in California, curiously, is the climate. It's not all palm-fringed beaches and sun so bright that Edna Everage sun specs must be worn at all times. Mark Twain said that the coldest winter he had ever spent was summer in San Francisco . . . a fog bank sitting over the ocean is sucked in by the heat of the inland valleys during the late afternoon, dropping the temperature where it sits by $40°$ to $50°F$. And these pockets of relative cool and shade are the most highly rated by wine-makers.

Left to their own devices, grapes will grow riper and sweeter – and quicker – in hot sun. That may sound like good news for wine-makers, but in fact grapes that are too ripe and which have ripened too quickly make big, blousy, highly alcoholic, uninteresting wines. What is needed is a protracted growing season, during which time the grapes have to struggle a bit to ripen. Then they will make subtle, stream-lined, enjoyable wines that will continue to improve as they mature.

Compare, for an instant, the grape with the apple. Those cotton-wool puff balls called Golden Delicious (generally from France) in the supermarkets are woolly and boring and uninteresting when compared with the fresh English Cox. The Cox grew slowly, struggling to make it to acceptable supermarket size during a patchy summer, and the flavours were concentrated marvellously as a result. To make good wine, it is better to have the struggling Cox sort of fruit.

Modern wine-making methods have, to an extent, redressed the shortcomings of over-generous weather. But it still remains that the absolute best wines will generally come from the cooler areas. Of course, there are subtle taste differences between different wines made from the same grape variety in different parts of California. Equally there are differences between wines made in the same place by different wine-makers. But there is a common theme. So I will describe the taste of a typical wine made from each of the different varieties (generally wines are made from a single variety in California) and then give a brief run-down of the places that give their names to the wine label so that you can make a stab at predicting what sort of quality/style to expect from any given bottle.

There are strict controls on the information allowed to be specified on the label, which work slightly like France's *Appellation Contrôlée*, although the only thing 'controlled' is the precise area specified. The most basic wines you're likely to see in Britain will state simply that they come from California (although legally they may include 25 per cent from another state). If at least 75 per cent of the grapes come from a particular county (such as Sonoma), this may be stated. More precise origins for the grapes, such as Russian River within the county of Sonoma, are also now recognised as 'Approved Viticultural Areas', and may also be boasted on the label. Being more specific as to the precise origins of the grapes is not necessarily a presumed bonus, as it is in the French *appellation* system, however.

The Grapes and Their Taste:

Cabernet Sauvignon

Until California entered the arena, it was presumed that serious Cabernet Sauvignon wines always had to have high levels of tannin (the ingredient that makes your tongue curl at the corners and leaves a drying feel in the mouth), and had to be kept for a long time before they softened sufficiently to be pleasant to drink. But the fecund soils and coaxing heat of California encouraged a buxom richness to develop in the fruit which translated (if left uncurbed) directly into the wine. California Cabernets were almost instantly likeable, wine-makers making much of the fruit and managing to contain the tannins to leave a light, juicy-fruity taste in the mouth. Because claret is the blueprint of Cabernet wines, though, increasingly wine-makers tried to restrain the forwardness of the fruit and introduce a sterner, firmer core. Both styles – that is the voluptuous and accessible original California style, and the quasi Bordeaux – exist on the shelves side by side. They are generally instantly distinguishable by price: the more challenging claretesque styles being more expensive.

At their simplest (i.e. cheapest) these red wines are juicy-fruity blackcurrant punnets without a single stern dimension in sight. Sounds great, you may say, but actually simple fruit craves some sort of backbone to pin it down. They can also be surprisingly light, with a piercing – almost eye-watering – acidity. Denser, maturer versions can throw up chocolatey flavours. Although the labels invariably state just Cabernet Sauvignon, there may well, as in claret, be some Merlot and/or Cabernet Franc in there too (remember, the wine-maker can put in 25 per cent without having to say so).

Chardonnay

Wherever it goes (and it has travelled a lot), the Chardonnay behaves slightly differently. In California the style is controlled voluptuousness . . . 'controlled', as in Burgundy and 'voluptuous' as in Australia. To achieve the controlled side of things, containing the rich, succulent tendencies of fully sun-ripe Chardonnay, the grapes are often picked before they get to that stage, which contributes a green-leaf tinge to the bouquet – a bit like angelica. But be not deceived, these are not slight 'green' wines; the alcohol is frequently a thunderous 13 per cent, giving richness and density. There is frequently a haunting floweriness tucked away in the taste, the pungence of honeysuckle and clover and the sweet sugary scents of a stick of seaside rock. Usually either fermented or matured (at least in part) in new oak, you can expect the associated vanilla notes, the appetising aroma of French patisserie. Too much wood, though, and the bouquet has slightly oily connotations. Too much sun, and you can get a whiff of boiled sweets and kiwi fruit. In the best orchestrations, although there is a strong suggestion of sweetness, a bit like the sugary coating of tinned travel sweets, once you have a taste from the glass you are instantly reassured that this white wine, although big and ripe, is also streamlined and dry.

Merlot

Plantings of the second great Bordeaux grape are comparatively small and much Merlot is engulfed by wines calling themselves Cabernet Sauvignon, where it anonymously contributes richness and concentration.

The grape is occasionally seen operating in its own right, when you will find that velvet is the immediate memory trigger. Rich berry fruits are recalled by this red wine, but without that piercing acidity you often find in Californian Cabernet Sauvignons. The nearest you get to a 'sharp' taste is with the slight association with damsons.

Pinot Noir

The red grape behind all the best red Burgundies and Champagnes hasn't taken very kindly to being uprooted and dragged around the world. Except in exceptional wines (which could play havoc with your bank balance), so far Pinot Noir has largely been a bit of a disappointment. In California it's been discovered that it must be given the coolest spots and then it will perform with suitable reticence and an increasing measure of real style.

In the best examples, you get that characteristic strawberry aroma – with overtones of compost. Don't be put off, the illustrious Pinot Noir often smells a bit like rotting vegetables, that's all part of the complex taste picture. Juicy berry fruit is the thing, with the merest prickle of lively acidity – too much acidity and the whole medley is blown and you're left with an inappropriately fizzy feeling in the mouth. But the days of too much fizz seem happily to be passing fast. Watch out Burgundy!

Sauvignon Blanc/Fumé Blanc

The Sauvignon is, of course, the grape behind the best Loire whites such as Sancerre and Pouilly-Fumé . . . the latter, traditionally, being a wood-aged Sauvignon of nutty, buttery loveliness, heavily fancied (and because of huge demand, subsequently ruined) by the American market. When Californian wines called simply Sauvignon

Blanc were having a tough time being accepted at home (the name, and the generally sugary-sweet style had become rather unfashionable) so Robert Mondavi coined the name 'Fumé Blanc' for his dry wood-matured Sauvignon made in the Napa Valley, and it stuck and was soon to become heavily plagiarised. The use of the name is quite arbitrary, however, and tells you nothing about the style of the wine (bar that it will be dry, in common with all Californian Sauvignon Blancs these days).

It may be either green and zippy or, generally from hotter areas, rich and generous. There is a slightly unripe taste to the first streamlined style, sometimes with twiggy or even tar-like connotations. Be prepared to be put in mind of the gooseberry again – either raw and unripe or stewed. There is an attractive lively zing to these spritely Sauvignons; a brightness and attractive mouthwash cleanness. In contrast, the oaky style may be more in line with asparagus on the taste spectrum – asparagus tart in fact, with the soft, buttery pastry notes coming in as well. And incidentally asparagus, that most difficult of foods to match with wine, wouldn't be a bad choice of dish to serve with them either.

Zinfandel

California's most widely planted red grape has a rags-to-riches story attached. Red Zinfandel wines used to be widely seen around simply because the grapes were so widely planted; now the area under vine is fully justified. The grape is not only responsible for some of America's darkest, densest, most idiosyncratic reds, but for a whole range of wines which have each earned their own fan clubs.

You need your hand held to an extent when buying a wine called Zinfandel. It can be inky and dense, or it can be light and fruity, even sweet and 'white' . . . or rather pink. The traditional rich, dark style is perhaps the most successful (although no longer the most fashionable), bringing a lovely penetrating spring-like quality to a heavyweight wine. The fruit can be mouth-wateringly piercing, and there's often an unmistakable scent of damp moss. Partnering traditional Zinfandels with food calls out for traditional food; none of your nouvelles are needed here, instead down to earth casseroles and roasts.

White Zinfandel

Wine styles bob in and out of fashion in America as often as the mini skirt. In the early to mid seventies, white wines were booming; the punters couldn't get enough of them. So wine-makers endeavoured to make as much white wine as possible and to call anything that resembled white wine in style 'white' as well. So 'White' Zinfandel is made like a white wine from the swashbuckling red grape, the Zinfandel, and because the skins are jam-packed with colour, the wine comes out to be not in fact white, but a pretty blush pink instead. It was discovered almost by accident. The Sutter Home winery specialised in just two styles: red Zinfandel and a sweet white Muscat. Considering diversifying, they experimented with simply producing a hybrid of the two (and the Muscat doesn't have to be declared on the label if it accounts for less than 25 per cent). So came about the birth of White Zinfandel. Creating a pretty, easy-drinking, aperitif style of wine from California's most widely-planted grape was a wizard marketing idea; it's now the best selling Californian wine on the home market.

Almost always erring on the semi-sweet side, White Zin (as it is called) locks up many of the scents and flavours of a confectionery counter. I have been put in mind of blackcurrant fruit pastilles, crystallised rose petals, sculpted sugar shapes, new mown hay and the heady scents of a spring garden by a whiff of White Zinfandel. The drier versions (such as Robert Mondavi's) bear a strong resemblance to elderberries. It's curious that such a 'serious' red wine grape could make such an unwiney wine. It must be served really well chilled and probably is best on its own, outdoors. A brilliant barbecue number and for mixed age groups.

☷ Sonoma County   ▦ Central Coast
⫽ Napa Valley   including Monterey
▤ Central Valley
                ▨ South Central Coast

Major Wine-producing Areas:

Of all the grape-growing regions of the Golden State, the marvellously pretty Napa Valley probably rings more bells in Britain than most, even though it's actually the smallest premium wine-producing region, with the smallest output of wine. If a wine comes from the Napa Valley, or the neighbouring Sonoma Valley, you can bet good money you'll see it emblazoned on the label; these are buzz words in California wine circles. But there are many other districts noted for their wines, divided into well over a hundred much more precise 'Approved Viticultural Areas'. Regrettably, from the point of view of peddling easy information to you, where the wine-maker deems his area to be 'unsexy', he keeps it off the label and boasts instead of the small AVA, which may or may not make you any the wiser.

For this reason, going systematically through the districts is not entirely relevant. Instead I'll list more 'buzz' names likely to be associated with the best wines.

Napa

This wide, flat-floored valley carpeted with vines and flowers runs north-east from San Francisco. Highly prized (and priced) vineyards are planted from the valley floor up to 1500 feet, so spanning the coolest temperatures California can do, up to the warm average for the state. Here many of the most famous names are concentrated – many hand-crafted wines and few bargain prices.

Sonoma County

Don't get confused. Sonoma County is the *district* spanning half a dozen valleys, including Sonoma *Valley*, a recherché little AVA. Prices for wines bearing this name are climbing steeply, although output is of fairly mixed quality (owing to varying microclimates, among other things). Some of the best wines will boast their Viticultural Area large and clear, with Russian River leading, followed by Alexander Valley and Dry Creek.

Monterey

A cool pocket of a southern grape sprawl south of San Jose, this is home to many of the big names of Californian wine, such as Paul Masson. The district within which Monterey falls, the Central Coast, is associated with mass-produced high tech wines, although 'boutique' wineries are following the big boys now too.

South Central Coast

This includes San Luis Obispo, Santa Barbara, Edna Valley, Santa Ynez and Santa Maria. Although the most southerly wine-producing district, the South Central Coast has a generous share of the coolest vineyards and plenty of talented wine-makers to make the most of them. These AVAs on the label generally spell top quality wines.

South America

Chile

 BRITAIN IS THE BIGGEST market for wine in the world. It's not that we are terrific drinkers – compared with Continental Europe our consumption is pretty puny – but our appetite for the new and the different is unequalled anywhere. If you lived in France, you would drink French wine, and not just *any* French wine, but wine made locally. Likewise if you lived in Australia, your vinous diet would be almost exclusively Australian. But living in Britain, you have the pick of wines from the whole world.

Not being particularly impressive wine producers in our own right, we have always had to buy our wine from abroad, and have become used to being offered an extremely wide choice. Historically, we have always had the pick of nearby Europe at our disposal, countless wines from France, Germany, Italy, Spain and Portugal; but still not entirely contented, our roving eye started looking further afield, falling on North America, South Africa, Eastern Europe, Australia, the Lebanon. Hardly a wine-producing country (and virtually every country in the temperate world makes wine of some sort) escaped our attention as we quested for new, better, cheaper, more original thrills.

Just when it seems as though there isn't another single place to explore, then along comes a new surprise. And one of the latest to tease the imagination is Chile, that long, thin strip of a country hugging the Pacific coast of South America. The Chileans are hardly new to this wine-making business, however; far from it. The country has one of the longest viticultural traditions outside Europe – and very much in the European style, so the wine 'travels' well.

The Spanish conquistadors first introduced the vine to South America in the mid-sixteenth century and it flourished in perfect conditions. That was the start of the business, but not the gold seal on its success. That came in the mid-nineteenth century with the grand European tour. Rich mine owners, having made their mint, took themselves across the world to experience the delights of Europe – including the wine. They were so taken with its excellence that they returned with their trunks bulging with European vines. Now here is the miracle. These vine cuttings of all our old favourites, Cabernet Sauvignon, Riesling, Sauvignon Blanc, Gewürztraminer *et al*, were plucked from the European vineyards only twenty years before their total devastation by the beastly little louse, phylloxera.

The European vineyards – and those of the rest of the world, for it was a fearless traveller, this phylloxera – were gradually re-established after this total devastation, of course, but only by being grafted on to phylloxera-impervious rootstock from America. Somehow the Chilean vineyards never appealed to the wandering louse (one theory is that they have too high a water table for comfort), so the vines remain splendidly ungrafted and intact, living up to four times longer than their grafted European relations in some of the healthiest vineyards in the world. The warmth of the long day sun cut by cooling breezes from the Pacific Ocean and a dramatic drop in the night-time temperature make these vineyards rather special, a fact that hasn't escaped the attention of modern-day conquistadors such as Miguel Torres, the eminent Spanish wine-maker, and the French Domaine Rothschild who both have considerable wine-producing interests in Chile.

The wine region runs down the 'central valley' (more a plateau, really) carved up by the valleys of the rivers Aconcagua, Maipo, Cachapoal, Tinquiririca, Lontue and Maule, all of which are names that could appear on the label, so I hope you're paying attention! There are no complex classifications like those in France, however, but local marks of superiority evolved – such as the 'Don' or 'Dona' prefix which is intended to imply a lordly, exceptional quality. It wasn't thought this subtle system of implied quality would have such an impact on our own market, so for wines sold abroad, the lordly titles have been dropped.

Along with the spanking new equipment that has been thumped into all the major Chilean wineries, the relaxed Californian approach to labelling has been adopted, meaning you read only what you find. Although the most widely planted grape in Chile is the homespun Pais, accounting for a massive 35 per cent of production, wines reaching Britain are all made and named after familiar grape varieties. So on a Chilean wine label you will see the name of the producer, the name of a region, the name of the grape and, perhaps, a brand name.

One slight blot on the credentials, though, is that it has been found that some of the less scrupulous producers have tried to give nature a bit of a helping hand and been over-enthusiastic with the chemical additives. Nothing too serious, but a hiccup in the marketing plans nonetheless.

The Grapes and Their Taste:

Cabernet Sauvignon

After the local Pais, good old Cab Sauv is Chile's second most important grape. And they are positively bursting with pride for it (it trounced the Cabernet class at the '87 Paris wine olympiad). And when you try a glass of this red wine you'll find it's *almost* all there, *almost* pulls it off, but there's usually some hitch to perfection.

Essentially there are two different styles, easily discernible from the label, being the young and the old (look for the vintage date). At best, the young (made within the last three years) are direct and straightforward, with zingy Parma violet sweet scents and ripe fruitgum flavours, but that's not always the case. They can seem rather fuddled and wrapped up, frowsty, almost, like a bedroom with the windows and doors shut tight. Find a good older version (five years or more) and you'll spy meat and might smoothed down with the flavours from a fruit tart. But there can still be a component out of place, perhaps a hint of egginess or a whiff of dust. In style, Chilean Cabernet Sauvignon has more in common with Bordeaux than Australia, but still asserts its own individuality which, with more practice on the international market, will possibly fade. There was news in the press of 'illicit additives' in some Chilean Cabernet Sauvignons, perhaps they have accounted for the 'out of place' flavours. After a good clean-up operation, therefore, perhaps we can look forward to more straightforward wines.

A Cabernet Sauvignon rosé gushing with blackcurrant fruit is also available.

Because of their simplicity, good young Chilean Cabernets can be drunk on their own without food, or matched with light, summery meals such as quiches, cold meats and salad, whereas the meatier older styles definitely demand something more substantial in the meat line, such as roasts and even game.

Chardonnay

Despite Chile's Garden of Eden conditions, the buzz grape of the eighties and nineties has been something of a failure there. Cut down by a serious virus problem and yielding less than any other grape variety, wine-makers

Wine-growing area
Chile

had virtually given up on it, but nothing encourages perseverance more than fashion and demand, so many Chilean wine-makers have now decided to do their damnedest to overcome the problems and come up with some good Chardonnays. And they are having a measure of success (to the delight of the Americans who gobble up most of it).

Chilean Chardonnay is quite individual. The most notable thing about it is that it is incredibly soft and gentle without a hint of astringent acidity. That's not a great plus in serious wine terms, but it certainly makes for very easy-drinking white wine (which is also lower in alcohol than most traditional and new world Chardonnays, incidentally). With oak-aged Chardonnays (and most are), you'll find smoky bonfire notes on the bouquet, blended with soft buttercup and marigold scents. Gently fragrant, that's what these Chilean Chardonnays are, calling to mind bunches of flowers and baskets of fruit. And on the palate, sweetly buttery, the fragrance still lingering to suggest the taste of scented flowers; like flower petals dipped in sugar. Creamy, white-sauced dishes would be the best food partners to team them with and light creamy soups such as Vichyssoise – or serve them alone without food. They would make a good 'dry wine' introduction to 'medium-to-sweet' white wine lovers. Unfortunately, keen to give their buzzy Chardonnays a bit of a helping hand, certain unscrupulous producers got up to a bit of jiggery-pokery in 1990 which brought their name into some disrepute. However, rest assured, they did nothing that was harmful to health.

Gewürztraminer

There are not many of these around, so I'll be brief. Alsace's humdinger of a pungent, spicy white grape produces its own restrained version down in Chile, lighter on the nose with a rather fragile bouquet leading you into a curious mixture of grassy greenness overlaid with a noticeable coating of residual sugar; where Alsace Gewürztraminer, although dry, appears to be sweet-and-sour, Chile's is sweet . . . and yet green. Nothing can beat spicy Oriental dishes as a partner for this grape; this version would suit wine novices better than examples from Alsace.

151

Riesling

The Chileans have not got too excited about this grape variety either, introduced in the mid-nineteenth century; it has been too frugal with its yield for their liking. But they have continued to use it to make some pretty flowery white wines, dry, but with an unexpected spiciness to them and a sharp tang when you swallow.

Sauvignon Blanc

The Chileans pin their wine-making prowess to the mast of the Sauvignon Blanc. Priding themselves on clean, ripe fruit, they manage to capitalise on the crunchy, crisp aspects of the grape, while keeping its tendency towards mouth-puckering acidity at bay. There is a coaxingly fragrant quality to these wines, putting you in mind of lily of the valley soap, and the scent continues well into the taste. You'll probably find more fruity sweetness than you'd expect from many of their close relations from elsewhere in the world. Some are oak-matured, which contributes a fuller, slightly spicy, smoky flavour and gives you a bit more to chew on, a broader medley of flavours in the mouth. The oak-matured versions suggest food; great with asparagus and other powerful vegetable flavours, artichokes, for instance.

Argentina

 THE FORTUNES OF Argentinian wine have had a somewhat stormy ride in the affections of the British, through no fault of their own. As the fifth largest wine producer in the world after Italy, France, Spain and the Soviets, she's something of a dab hand at putting out well-priced juicy-fruity affordable plonk, and we used to lap it up before the dreaded Falklands War. When Her Majesty's battleships set sail for the South Atlantic, lakes of the stuff was either here already or on its way, and patriotically we turned our backs on the lot.

It has taken a long time for 'Argentinian' to cease to be an unacceptable word, even in wine circles, but slowly wines bearing this banner are creeping back – hooray! This time less in the guise of cheap and cheerful plonk, more as individuals to be judged on their own merits. But since the bulk of Argentinian wine is ordinary everyday stuff, perhaps some of that will follow on, too. After all we don't want all the geese on the shelves to aspire to be swans.

The three main areas are Mendoza, the biggest, concentrating on reds; San Juan, which is hotter and drier; and Rio Negro, which is small and promising. Of the rest only La Rioja is noteworthy, largely because being enormously hot, its wines bear no resemblance at all to its famous counterpart in Spain. Many of the international band of grape varieties are planted, along with national idiosyncrasies such as Criolla, which is responsible for making more millions of gallons than any other type. Blends are locally popular, the Heinz 57s of the wine world; but on Britain's wine shelves you will find wines made from individual grape varieties you will recognise, as well as the excellent spicy white Torrontes.

The Grapes and Their Taste:

Cabernet Sauvignon

There's a delightful simplicity to this red grape grown in Argentina, where it concentrates all its endeavours on putting out pure honest fruit. You get blackcurrants on the nose, blackcurrants on the taste; straightforward fruit flavours through and through with hardly a distraction bar the sort of drying tartness you find in unripe currant skins. But despite all this fruit, the wine is seriously dry – and it must be said, a shade one-dimensional. Put it with a good, rich bolognese sauce, or even a mild chilli con carne, and this will ink in the gaps missing in the wine and make a deliciously simple combination.

Wine-growing area
Argentina

Chenin Blanc

Low acidity and a bad case of blandness is a problem here. There's a bit of the dirty dishcloth syndrome, too, just to complete the condemnation. So it's not surprising you're more likely to find it operating in a white blend than striking out on its own.

Riesling

A good foil for the Chenin, above, with which it is often blended, the piercing floral notes add the zip required to perk up the Chenin's flabbiness, giving green, grassy scents with a touch of unripe melon to the white wine. The bouquet is more promising than the palate deserves, being a bit soapy with overtones of milk of magnesia. I won't make a food suggestion, because it needs to improve a bit before it is worth buying.

Torrontes

There is a haunting and elusive bouquet to this white wine, which has fleeting hints at sweet marshmallows and marzipan. After a sip you'll be transported to hot evergreen woods – a Mediterranean camp site, perhaps – by the pine scented flavour. There's a hint of tea rose in there, too, and a lingering taste of pine nuts. Although the wine is dry, it's very busy with lots going on; therefore it calls out for simple food as an accompaniment, nothing more complicated than simple grilled fish such as sole or roast chicken with plain trimmings.

Australia

THE CAPTAIN of the First Fleet sailing to Sydney two hundred years ago was a man after my own heart. Among his essential desert island rations he included some *vitis vinifera* wine-producing vines. Rushing to heel them into the soil as soon as possible, the first specimens were planted near the port in a place too hot and steamy for their own good. They didn't flourish, but replacements were acquired and taken further inland towards the now famous Hunter Valley to be established. Within a handful of years of colonisation, all the southern states had vineyards. And these sites still support vines today (though with the wisdom of hindsight, some are considered to be far from ideal, although the wonders of new wine-making technology are now well able to overcome any climatic shortcomings).

The Australian wine industry is of course a mere babe in arms compared with that in Europe. And the soil and climate are very different, too. Early wines tended, to put it mildly, towards the heavyweight class; massive, chunky reds and sticky, sweet whites, generally fortified with grape spirit. Adding grape spirit (the practice used for making sherry and port and such sweeties as Muscat de Beaumes de Venise) acts as a preservative, essential for wines that may have had to embark on the lengthy sea voyage half-way round the world back to the mother country (Australian wines were first exported to Britain in 1830). It also makes you rather drunk and gives you a headache if you drink too much of it; not a problem with early life-in-the-raw Australia, but as the society – and the wine-making methods – became more sophisticated, so the demand for delicate table wines increased.

The big switch began thirty years ago. Unencumbered by tradition, modern Australian wine-makers were able to start making their thoroughly modern table wines with a clean slate, and wholeheartedly embrace the new thinking and modern equipment emanating from the seats of learning in the northern hemisphere. Things moved apace, and now Australian table wines are a match (more than a match sometimes) for all the old favourites. They are easy to understand, usually named after the grape varieties from which they are made, and being forthcoming with positive bouquets and powerful flavours, they are easy to appreciate. Fortunately for us, they are now easy to find, too, and generally very competitively priced.

THE TASTE OF WINE

In the classic European regions, wine-makers, in common with other bods involved in agriculture, frequently complain about the weather. Will there be enough sun to bring their precious grapes to a sufficient state of ripeness to make good wine? In Australia, too, the weather can be a problem – but there too much heat and sun is the bugbear. Unless they are picked unnaturally early in the season, the grapes are *always* ripe. So instead of being reticent and shy, Australian wines are packed with fruit and flavour. You can usually spot an Australian wine at several paces; it's strong in colour, rich in bouquet and succulent in flavour.

Although wine is made in every Australian state, the bulk comes from the south-east – South Australia, New South Wales and Victoria – with comparatively small quantities being made near the south-west coast of Western Australia. Although Australian wine experts steeped to the gills in the native product can detect subtle differences between wines made in different locations from the same grape variety, the differences are very subtle; too subtle for the likes of us. So I am going to give you taste profiles of all the major grape varieties and offer thumb-nail sketches of the main wine-producing areas they come from (most areas grow most grape varieties), pointing out any magical marriages between the two which exist.

Australia's wines are principally based on eight main grape varieties. Many others are planted – some in quite large volume – but their progeny have made little impact on the wine shelves abroad. The information you find on Australian wine labels is also disarmingly straightforward. Most important is the grape variety (or varieties if it is a blend of two different grape types), almost invariably stated on the main label. If more than two different grape types are involved (as in the case of some blends sold under a brand name such as 'South Australia Red'), the grapes cannot be listed on the front label if the wine is sold in the EC; but they'll often be specified on the back label. In general, Australian wine labels are more helpful than most.

On the subject of blends, because Australia grows the classic and fashionable grape varieties in abundance, those types most commonly associated with fine (well finer than average anyway) wines in Europe, it is a mistake to sniff at an unspecified blend or brand. Like as not, a wine called simply South Australia Red will be a medley of varieties including some Cabernet and some Shiraz. A dry white will probably revolve around Rhine Riesling and a medium white around Chenin Blanc, Chardonnay, Sémillon and Muscadelle.

Also on the main label, you'll see the region the wine comes from, the name of the producer and, either on the front or back label, an indication of whether or not the wine has been fermented or matured in oak barrels (this affects the taste, so it's handy to know). There are no quality designations; unless you are familiar with the reputations of the various producers you have to let price labels speak for themselves (which they do fairly reliably).

The Grapes and Their Taste:

Cabernet Sauvignon

There can be a marvellous simplistic fruitiness (and how!) to Australia's version of the world's favourite red grape variety. Originally claret's own top grape, the Cab, as it is fondly called in Oz, has made itself at home in all Australia's wine areas, and makes marvellously fragrant, juicy-fruity up-front wines. Intensely purple in colour and intensely blackcurranty on the bouquet, there can be a beguiling ripeness, a forwardness and friend-liness to these wines unmatched by anything Europe can produce. At their simplest, they are undemanding fruit-pop wines, but usually the wine-maker packs in a serious edge, too. Fre-quently ageing the wine in oak, there can be a firm backbone in there, and the characteristic tough, drying flavours of tannin plus, of course, overtones of gentle, sweet vanilla. Green peppers have been associated with the taste, and occasionally eucalyp-tus. Big, blossoming rose-in-full-bloom wines can be made instinctively in Australia, but a snobbery is attached to managing to hone them more in the style of reticent, buttoned-up Bordeaux. To this end, the simplicity of the Cabernet Sauvignon is 'complicated' not only by wine-making twists, but also by the inclusion of a smidgen of the other clas-sic Bordeaux grapes of Merlot and Cabernet Franc. (If these represent less than 15 per cent of the whole, they may not be mentioned on the label.)

Cabernet Sauvignon/Shiraz

Cabernet Sauvignon has historically almost invariably been blended. There's not a classic claret made 100 per cent from this red grape; in many ways it's a new world preoccupation, producing single variety wines. But the Australians do also have the ability to be master blenders – their astonishingly popular cask or box wines can be veritable fruit salads. Among the classic varieties, this is an excellent combination.

Where Cabernet Sauvignons can be a bit one-dimensional – fruit and not a lot of substance to back it up – the Shiraz contributes might; and where the Shiraz can be just a bit *too* mighty, the Cabernet Sauvignon brings levity and bags of sweet, simple fruit. Like the ingredients in a recipe, the quantities in a blend can be adjusted to perfection. Not every blend is, though. Cheaper and own label versions can sometimes be a bit tough and stalky.

Chardonnay

There is a marvellous richness, a voluptuousness to Australian Chardonnay, unmatched anywhere else. In part this comes from the weather – unremitting hot sun during the growing period to produce plump, ripe, sugar-laden grapes. And in part from the fact that most Chardonnays from down under are matured in oak casks, if not actually fermented in them. These are BIG white wines, make no mistake.

You hardly need dip your nose down into the glass to breathe in the bouquet; it jumps up to meet you. The pervading sensation is buttery; you smell it, and feel it in the texture, even when you've only got as far as breathing in the bouquet; butter and honey and fruit. It is fruit with a difference, though, as in fruit in syrup, tinned mandarins or peaches, or even something more exotic, lychees, pawpaws and their ilk; rich, ripe and densely flavoured.

Whereas wood-ageing in red wines gives a hint of vanilla; coupled with ripe Chardonnay, the sensation is of creamy patisserie – with a tiny sprinkling of pencil shavings. The tendency is to give Australian Chardonnays quite a lot of contact with oak and when they are young, this gives a burning feeling in the mouth, a bit of a sting on the inside of the cheek, a smarting in the throat. In well-made examples, the fruit is enough to tone down the oak, and as the wine matures (three or four years) the two balance each other out beautifully. Although the bouquet is rich and the feel of the wine is rich, usually it is in fact quite dry. The fruity taste can appear to be swaddled in icing. It is mouth-filling and taste bud blowing; almost a meal in itself. To match it with food, don't go for the usual 'white wine options'; it would murder a limp fish pie. Oilier fish such as salmon stands up to the intensity, and so do rich pale meat dishes such as veal and escalopes of pork. You can put this sort of wine with cheese, but don't make the mistake of matching the apparent richness with desserts; sweet food makes it taste searingly dry.

Marsanne

The white equivalent of Syrah (Shiraz) in its native northern Rhône has travelled little beyond its natural habitat (where it contributes to white Crozes-Hermitage and makes white St-Joseph and St-Peray) but has rather bravely ventured to Australia where it is most widely seen in Victoria.

It is a very distinctive, solid grape variety invariably buttressed by wood. To look at, wood-aged Marsanne is intense yellow in colour. The bouquet that wafts off the glass of this amber nectar reminds me of hemp rope – the very natural sort with prickly loose fibres. It is fresh in a piney, sappy sort of way, an attractive astringence cutting through the otherwise rich, oily, buttery aromas. The astringence continues into the flavour, where it takes on the flavour of orange zest. There's a piney edge to the bone-dry taste, too.

Muscat

That marvellously pungent white grape from the same family as the Muscatel can be coaxed into many styles, though in every guise it retains its aromatic pot-pourri bouquet. Dry Muscats present quite a riddle to the old taste buds. On the nose, they seem sweet and spicy and rich, but on the palate that richness hones down into a dry-but-spicy pungence. 'Late picked' on the label indicates that the wine will be sweet, the grapes having been picked when they were dripping with sweetness and sugar. I can't dissociate the delicate, flowery taste of Muscat wines with munching through a gardenia petal sandwich (I never have, but once saw the recipe for the same in a copy of American *House and Garden* and can imagine it vividly). Chilled right down, it makes an interesting aperitif – good with salty nibbles, too.

Rhine Riesling

Germany's most highly rated grape variety, and one of the world's great aristocrats, is the most widely planted classic white wine grape in Australia, but you wouldn't guess it looking at Britain's wine shop shelves. As popular as Germany's white wines have been, Australia's version has failed to make much impact. But we're passing up some real treats.

As in Germany, the variety is vinified to make wines of various levels of sweetness, ranging from dry, through medium to sweet. The dry style proliferates, generally vinified to be a squeaky clean, crisp dry white. There is a gentle floral whiff to the bouquet, a sappy 'green' quality – almost a vibrance; this wine seems to be thoroughly alive – and a suggestion of oiliness; the slightest scent of an aeroplane revving up (a very distinctive memory trigger for the Riesling, incidentally). On the taste, there is the pungent recollection of flowers and a sweet fruitiness, topped with honey. Pricier examples are aged in oak, which contributes richness in taste and body. But despite it all, the impression of greenness is the most lasting one. Rhine Rieslings are useful chaps to have about, being good drink-on-their-own wines (very well chilled) and accommodating partners for white meat dishes – even those with powerfully flavoured sauces.

Sauvignon Blanc

The escalating thirst we (and much of the civilised world) have for steely, slim dry white wines has turned Australia's attention to the little darling of the Loire, the Sauvignon Blanc (sometimes called Fumé Blanc, when the wine has noticeably been matured in wood, a fashion begun in California). Until the mid eighties, Chardonnay had the lion's share of Australian white wines to itself; but Sauvignon's contribution is growing apace.

The Sauvignon grape is all gooseberries to me ... but with the generous rations of sun in Oz, often coupled with a kiss of oak, the pungence softens, the caramelly tones of the oak come to the fore, and the gooseberries take on an easy stewed-with-sugar character. A much bigger, fatter, softer version of the Loire's Pouilly Fumé.

Semillon

In Australia, the traditional grape of both sweet and dry white Bordeaux behaves much like the rich-but-dry Chardonnays (with which it is often blended); it can be difficult to spot the two apart at times. So it's another big, rich, buttery thunderbolt (if that's not a contradiction in terms!) with the fleeting scent of egg custard. The appearance is of baled straw in colour, and appropriately so, since the scent of hay or damp straw is a familiar one with these wines. Again, nose in glass, you get an inhalation of pure honey with a whiff of toast. There is fruit there, too, in abundance, mangoes perhaps if you search hard enough. The taste is soft – blousy almost – and soothingly smooth (although the wood can bite, if too raw). Semillon was one of the early stars of the Hunter Valley, made to be aged for years, when it assumed the flavour of nuts and honey – and the name, curiously, of Hunter River Riesling (at the time it was difficult to sell under its own name). Now (under the proper name of Semillon) it's generally made to peak earlier, and fermenting or ageing in new oak casks inks in the features formerly contributed by old age. It doesn't enjoy so much fame and acclaim as Chardonnay, although in many cases it deserves to. Good food wine – anything and everything really, in the positive flavour line.

Semillon/Chardonnay or Chardonnay/Semillon Blends

The dominant grape in the blend is the first to be mentioned and dictates the style of the wine. Lean Chardonnays (for Australia, that is) are filled out by the generous Semillon, which is big on body and flavour and tends to be lighter on acidity. A very happy marriage, this one, between like minds.

Shiraz

The Shiraz is known as the Syrah in Europe where it is most famous for its contribution to the great wines of the Rhône. In Australia, it is the most widely planted red variety. In the early days – and there were about 170 years of 'early days' before the new era dawned and wine-makers started making table wines seriously for the first time – grapes that presented few difficulties in either the vineyard or the winery were favoured, and those that made good fortified wines were favoured most. Enter the Shiraz. Fortunately for 'new era' wine-makers, it also makes good, individual table wine.

I've got to get straight to the point on the taste of this one. The Australian memory trigger for the Shiraz says it all. They liken it (on the nose, at least) to a sweaty saddle. Okay, so maybe you haven't

come across many of those in your time, but use
your imagination. Think of supple leather newly
cleaned with creamy saddle soap, if you can, and
add that slight 'dirty feet' whiff you get off some
southern French wines. You've also got to add the
dimension of fruit, of course, Australian wine's
great talking point. And there you have a rough outline of the Shiraz. This grape is capable of making
big, meaty thunderbolts, inky dark, tarry, muscular and solid. There's a spiciness to them as well, a
peppery feeling in the throat. Carbonade of beef
they can call to mind; meat cooked in beer . . . with
perhaps some redcurrant jelly on the side – and
that wouldn't be a bad food accompaniment.
They're up to any spicy, hefty meals you can dream
up, classically good with game – venison a winning
partner.

Main Wine-producing Areas:

New South Wales

With Sydney as its capital, NSW was the first state to have vines, and the Hunter
Valley, three hours' drive north from Sydney, was the first area to make an impact on
British wine drinkers.

Hunter Valley   Beautiful and tranquil though this prestige wine-producing area
is, with its hills and rivers, trees and very varied vegetation, it wouldn't be chosen now
as an ideal site for vines, it's much too hot. But it was one of the very first areas where
vineyards flourished and vines have remained there ever since. The heat, however,
can be overcome by modern technology, and it's certainly not unusual to find
mechanical harvesters at work in the middle of the night, picking while the grapes are
cool. The reputation of Hunter wines is high in Britain – and sometimes for the wrong
wines! Australian connoisseurs would tip Sémillon and Shiraz as the best varieties for
the area; some good Chardonnays come from there, too, but it's not so highly rated for
Cabernet Sauvignons.

Riverina   The official name for the vast fruit farming planes directly west of
Sydney by some five hours' drive is the unromantic sounding Murrumbidgee Irrigation Area. And unromantic, I suppose, it is, being principally a volume producer and
the great provider of the domestic 'bladder pack' (alias wine box). Irrigation is not the
dirty word in Australia that it is in European wine circles, and highly sophisticated
methods make fruit flourish in virtual desert conditions. Unusually dry, light, juvenile
Sémillons from here are worth looking out for (though because Riverina is known as a
bulk wine-producing area, the label may coyly say South Eastern Australia instead).

162

Mudgee This aboriginal word means 'little nest in the hills', and it's very pretty and just that. Protected by altitude from that great thwack of heat suffered by the other wine areas in the state, Mudgee enjoys cool nights and a longer ripening period than the Hunter – the harvest is an astonishing month later. And consequently it boasts better, more precisely defined flavours. Best known for her reds: Cabernet and rich and chocolatey Shiraz.

South Australia

Australia's most important wine state, South Australia produces more than half her output.

Barossa Valley To the north of Adelaide, this spacious, comfortable valley twenty miles long, surrounded by ranges of hills – even with the odd 'peak' – is home to a wine business with very Germanic beginnings (and 'continuings', too). Lutheran immigrants fleeing persecution at home set forth for the agnostic farms of Barossa. But understanding more about the habits of the vine, they quickly turned to wine-making instead. They spoke their own language (Barossa Deutsch), patented their own Barossa *wurst* and dotted the landscape with picture postcard churches. Not surprisingly, the most widely planted grape here is the Rhine Riesling, although this suffered a bit of a popularity set-back in the seventies, and pockets of Riesling vineyards gave way to the deeply fashionable Chardonnay, which makes a particularly floral, streamlined wine here with a suggestion of honeysuckle. All styles of wine are made in the Barossa, with the Cabernet Sauvignons and Cab/Shiraz blends being particularly distinguished and finely honed. Good quality at reasonable prices.

Clare Valley Stone wall fringed lanes wind through this little Utopia famous for its Rhine Rieslings in good German style; floral and petrolly. Good also for Shiraz.

Coonawarra 'Flat and featureless' is how contemporary Australians describe Coonawarra, four hours' drive south of Adelaide, a gift of an area for making red wines (eat your heart out Bordeaux!). The soil is perfect, the climate cooled by the proximity to the coast, and the water table is reassuringly close and consistent, bringing in scores of wine-makers to the area whose vineyards and wineries are packed chock-a-block into the valley. Cabernets (often blended with either of the other main claret grapes) are refined (though expensive), Shiraz consistently good and the tricky Pinot Noir settling down to reassure its proponents.

Padthaway An overspill vineyard area from fecund Coonawarra twenty-five miles up the road, it is equally propitious, but favoured more for white varieties, Sauvignons, Chardonnay and Rhine Riesling.

Riverland Over towards the New South Wales border, you have South Australia's answer to Riverina – Riverland, a hot, plain plane, highly irrigated to produce essentially 'bulk' wines, mostly destined for wine casks. They used to be distilled for spirit, but their climb up the ladder of quality is now aspiring more towards producing bottled varietals named after individual grapes. Southern France's Grenache works well with Shiraz for some well-priced reds. Good value in the main.

McLaren Vale   This is a picture postcard coastal region with patchwork of vine-yards, meadows and, of course, nearby, the beach. Generally small volumes and high prices, but high standards, too.

Victoria

Vineyards are scattered all over the state of Victoria – some areas, such as Milawa, supporting only one producer, Brown Brothers, who send a lot of good stuff over to Britain. Brown Brothers have made a speciality of concentrating on the individual varieties, and plant their vineyards at different heights up the hills depending on the sensitivity of the grapes concerned. Everything is planted in Victoria . . . somewhere. It is dubbed the Garden State, enjoying cooler weather than most of the country and an interesting (to say the least) weather pattern; it can rain, snow, and shine brilliantly all on the same day, in the same place. Among the varied flora, eucalyptus abound, and it has been said they contribute a 'minty' taste to the wine. Goulburn, about sixty miles north of Melbourne, hosts the unusual and delicious white variety Marsanne, along with good Sauvignons (called Fumé Blancs if aged in oak). Yarra prides itself on having some highly prestigious 'boutique' (i.e. tiny) wineries, commanding enormous prices. At the other end of the production scale, Mildura is Victoria's answer to Riverland; in fact it's actually an extension of Riverland, putting out volumes of accessibly priced plonk.

Western Australia

Calling itself the State of Excitement (much to Eastern Australia's amusement), this is a remote area of wine production in the Perth environs, from where sales to Sydney are even classed as 'export'. Good wines of all qualities emanate from valleys heading for the sea.

Swan Valley   Swan Valley has the reputation for being the hottest successful grape-growing region in the world. The best known Swan producer in Britain is Houghton, who harness the climate to do great things. Chenin Blanc is important and they miraculously manage to make lightweight versions of both Chardonnay and Semillon (Burgundy is definitely the role model).

Margaret River   A beautiful seaside region favoured by prestigious boutique wineries, the Chardonnays are Burgundian here, the Semillons herbaceous and grassy, though Shiraz wines tend to be rather unexciting.

Mount Barker   By contrast to the Swan, this area is cool and much more remote. Good-looking European-style wines (Plantagenet made by an Englishman), but not much about in the UK yet; worth waiting for.

Blended Wines

Sometimes, just to confound the simplicity of the wines coming from these individual areas, grapes from several areas – even several states – may be included in a wine. Australian wine-makers think nothing of lugging grapes or grape juice huge distances to make up a particular blend. Obviously the wine may not then lay claim to a small individual area. It may instead call itself something general like South East Australia (an umbrella name including all wine-producing states bar Western Australia). Don't be put off. Again, this is not a black mark against the wine. It simply means some wine-makers search far afield for the right grapes for their blends (or so they'd have you believe).

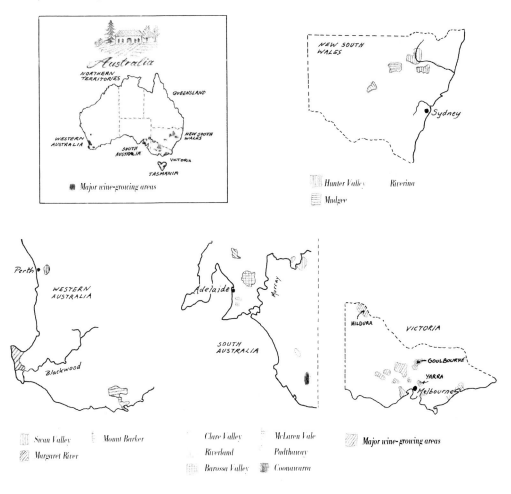

Major wine-growing areas

Hunter Valley   Riverina
Mudgee

Swan Valley   Mount Barker
Margaret River

Clare Valley   McLaren Vale
Riverland   Padthaway
Barossa Valley   Coonawarra

Major wine-growing areas

New Zealand

WINE USED TO BE a local thing, rather like vegetables, I suppose. If you didn't grow beans yourself, you'd buy them from someone in the village who did. And you'd buy your wine from the nearest producer, too. This was a bit easier for the French than the Brits, I'll grant you, but we still mainly shopped locally – as locally as possible in the case of wine – for all provisions.

But no more. And there's no greater evidence of how things have changed than the fact that Britain is the largest market abroad for New Zealand wines, made as far around the world as is technically possible. Now, at the beginning of the nineties, more than a hundred different New Zealand wines are on sale on British wine shop shelves . . . which is a hundred more than there were at the beginning of the eighties. As far as Britain is concerned, New Zealand wines have only just been born, but coming from much the same sort of climate as our own (okay then, quite a bit sunnier, I'll admit) and from vineyards planted in countryside that bears a close resemblance to our own as well, we feel at home with them. To put it in the words of the Trade Commissioner at New Zealand House, there has been 'significant receptivity here to the character, elegance and value of our cool climate varietals' . . . or in my own words: they are definitely our sort of wines.

New Zealand's wine industry in fact dates back to the early days of colonisation just over a hundred and seventy years ago (*vitis vinifera* the wine-making grape is European and had to be carried to the southern hemisphere aboard ship). In common with France, New Zealand has no dried fruit business; she's not into raisins and sultanas. What sort of statistic is that, you might ask? Well it's a significant one, as it happens, meaning two things. First that the only purpose for growing grapes (other than for the table) is for making wine, so wine-making varieties have always dominated. And second that the climate is a thoroughly temperate one. For sultanas you need heat, for wine, moderation.

New Zealand wines very much follow classic European styles. The most widely planted grape variety is Germany's Müller-Thurgau, although you wouldn't guess it by looking at your local supermarket's wine shelves; it's almost exclusively vinified into easy drinking plonk for the domestic market and as that market, too, becomes more sophisticated, so Müller-Thurgau's slice of the action is slimming down. Next in importance come the two French aristocrats, Chardonnay and Cabernet Sauvignon, with Sauvignon Blanc following not far behind. In order to prove herself to the world as a premium wine-maker, New Zealand largely concentrates on these three French varieties, but she also makes a good line in Chenin Blanc, Gewürztraminer, Rhine Riesling (much of which is 'late picked' to make sweet treats), Pinot Noir and South Africa's Pinotage, a highly successful cross between the Pinot Noir and the Cinsaut.

The Grapes and Their Taste:

Cabernet Sauvignon

Shall I compare thee to a traditional claret? Thou art more mouth-watering and less tough. These are juicier, fruitier versions of the old red favourite from nearer home, and so less demanding as a result. The fruit is as intense as a punnet of freshly picked redcurrants, as easy drinking as the juice from them just starting to ferment. Although you get redcurrants by the wheelbarrow load off these wines, there is another thoroughly individual taste of rose-hips, as well. If you've ever nibbled a rose-hip (and if you haven't and you're thinking of it in the future, let me warn you now, nibble only on the very edge – a big bite and you have a mouthful of hair shirt) you'll recollect the sweetness and the tart tannic tones in medley, and that's just what you find here. The scents and flavours of cassis, too, seem to be lurking in some examples. If you are looking for faults with these wines, it is in their simplicity; they can be like punnets of fruit without much substance or body to back it up. And the fruit isn't always succulent and inviting, it can taste a bit raw and unripe.

Chardonnay

If you could choose only one adjective to describe all New Zealand wines, it would have to be herbaceous. You don't have to look far in any of her white wines to find a leafy green flavour lurking under the fruit; and Chardonnay is no exception. Although New Zealand is definitely 'new world' in wine terms, and the style of her wines has that characteristic new world forwardness, there is an element of the reticent old world about them too.

Certainly she can make some big, rich, peachy Chardonnays *à la* Australia if she tries, but delicate balance is more the thing, streamlining the grape with a measure of astringence. The tendency for the grapes to be rich and ripe produces fruit flan flavours, fruity and buttery with the strong scent of grape juice, but this is balanced by a flinty, gunpowdery edge, reminiscent of sparklers or flaring matches. Oak barrels are generally used either to ferment or mature the wines, and contribute predictable buttery, vanilla flavours. Other nuances to look out for are that broad, flat scent of old Champagne and the merest suggestion of junipers. Without being too big or blousy, the richer style of NZ Chardonnay manages to be as mouth-coating as possible while still remaining totally dry.

Sauvignon Blanc

Sauvignon Blanc is the wine of which New Zealanders are justifiably most proud. They are thoroughly individual, these Sauvignons, with more natural woomph than examples from the Loire, but not so much that they lose their bite. It almost goes without saying that they are leafy green – a typical characteristic of both the Sauvignon grape and of New Zealand wines which becomes positively verdant in combination – but they are much more besides. You could find red peppers in there, even a whiff of chillies, bracken, lemon, geraniums, herbaceous flowers, swamp plants . . . plus, of course, the inevitable gooseberry/cat character given off by the Sauvignon Blanc, but this time it is coddled in cotton wool. And the medley of fruits and flavours is all served up with a rapier directness; the green flavours are so green they almost hurt. But there is also an unusual richness and depth to these wines, often acquired without the helping hand of oak barrels, which puts them in a class of their own. The body and richness intensifies as the wines mature; most are sold and enjoyed young, but keep them for a few years and they take on the smell and taste of asparagus soup (which, if you think of it, is in the same family, taste-wise, as the gooseberry).

The Main Wine-producing Areas:

Settlers in a new land have too much on their mind to worry too much about precisely where to site the first vineyards. Convenience is usually a higher priority than climate, and so in New Zealand, in common with much of the new world, the oldest established vineyards are not necessarily the best. Vine growing and wine-making in New Zealand got off to rather a shaky start, the damp being a difficult element to counter. But thirst spurred on the more scientifically minded to persevere, and gradually Auckland and Hawke's Bay, both on the North Island, were established as the first main centres. Of these, Hawke's Bay still flourishes, although attention has largely turned from Auckland to drier, sunnier spots further south.

Although the mounting onslaught from New Zealand wines on the wine shop shelves in Britain might suggest otherwise, the New Zealand wine industry is in fact pretty small by comparison, say, with that of Australia. But this is not because there is insufficient suitable land to plant. Far from it. As the tractors and ploughs work to prepare further planting areas, they are making furrows in virgin soil never before cultivated. And there's no shortage of virgin soil. The main players in the export field consider New Zealand's potential in our market to be limitless, as limitless as the hundreds of miles of rolling acres of verdant land at present exploited only by sheep. Most areas accommodate most grape varieties, although there are special partnerships worth shouting about.

Hawke's Bay

The undulating contours of this pretty, sheltered area inland from the south-east coast of the North Island, were one of the first successful areas to be planted and have deservedly retained their traditional importance, especially for Cabernet Sauvignon, the second most planted grape (to Müller-Thurgau, that is) which produces restrained French style wines here. Hawke's Bay Chardonnays are renowned, too, in the ripe, peachy style.

Gisbourne

Primarily a volume producer for the home market from vines carpeting the flat valley floors, Gisbourne struggles under an unglamorous image. But a few white treats emanate from selected vineyards, particularly Gewürztraminer. Gisbourne is considered the tops where this marvellously spicy, sweet-and-sour grape from Alsace is concerned. Müller-Thurgau dominates in volume terms, with Muscat close behind, although Chardonnay is up there with the big boys, occasionally scoring highly as in Villa Maria's Reserve aged in oak.

Marlborough

Only within the last twenty years has this area to the north of the South Island suc-
cumbed to the vine. And, nestling as they appear to in English countryside, vines like
it here a lot. It is undoubtedly a premium area of the future especially for all white
grape varieties, lending itself most distinctively to New Zealand's own thoroughly
individual style of Sauvignon Blanc.

Wine-growing areas

South Africa

WINES HAVE BEEN made in South Africa's Cape region for three-and-a-half centuries now. Indeed she's one of the world's big producers (though you'd certainly never guess it from looking at the wine shelves in Britain or any other wine-consuming country in the world). For, although massive volumes of wine are made, more than half is distilled into brandy, and the remaining table wine has a tough – in many countries an impossible – job finding a market. So the Cape wine industry has to make its way virtually isolated from the outside world.

Traditionally, South Africa was known for her fortified wines, and it is only since the late fifties that table wines have come to the fore; fortified port and sherry types dominated before. New technology introduced at that time pitched South Africa swiftly into the international arena with her new light wines, and in the sixties and early seventies she was generally considered to be ahead of her new world rivals America and Australia, both technically and on the quality scale. Her wines were marketed on their own merits and not as were so many others at that time, as French wine clones. Things looked good for this Garden of Eden of a country, but only briefly. It wasn't long before she started her rapid slide into the background, precipitated first by the nit-picking Afrikaner mentality and swiftly endorsed by economic sanctions imposed by so much of the world.

Where other competing nations in the brave new world market that was opening up used every ingenuity they could dream up to tailor their wines to meet specific demands – by switching vineyard after vineyard, for instance, from locally loved varieties to those with more international appeal – vine growers in South Africa were denied access to the buzz grape types and had to make do with what they already had.

And with the imposition of sanctions, the wine industry became even further removed from the real world. Australia and America took the lead with New Zealand, leaving South Africa trailing way way behind. Although the popular classic grape varieties are being used now, wines produced from them and from the traditional South African types seem somehow to straddle traditional and squeaky-clean new wave wines in style; whites, although clean, can be rather washed out and characterless, while reds, although boasting fruit born of the now not-so-new technology, acquire tough, meaty characteristics from prolonged captivity in old oak casks.

Wines most frequently encouraged to travel tend to be based on Chenin Blanc (called Steen in South Africa) for whites, and Cabernet Sauvignon for reds, backed up by a small show for Pinotage, a successful native crossing of Pinot Noir and Cinsaut, and the odd unspecified blend. The main exporter is KWV (Ko-operatieve Wijnbouwers Vereniging), the government-controlled national co-operative organisation.

Although in Britain there are no offcial sanctions against South African wine, there is a certain customer resistance to them and they are sold without any kind of promotion in the high street and are little seen on restaurant wine lists and neighbours' dining tables. As incentives to stock them at all, good price deals are struck, although, bearing in mind how cheap labour is in South Africa compared with in the rival countries, the financial squeeze is probably less punishing on the producers than it could appear.

The Wines and Their Taste:

Cabernet Sauvignon

There's no mistaking the red grape here; blackcurrant fruit races up your nose in a sharp searing way at first sniff, followed promptly by the slight whiff of tupperware. On the taste, there's plenty of sweet juicy fruit, but with the plasticky edge persisting – giving the impression you are drinking from a plastic cup. There's an edginess to the wine; the right ingredients appear to be here, but out of balance. Swallowing leaves a jangling, slightly metallic feel on the tongue.

Chenin Blanc

There's a definite citrusy edge to South African Chenins, like a whiff of fresh-peeled grapefruit tinged with the suggestion of concentrated orange juice with its slightly cooked, artificial connotations. A hint of sugary sweetness is to be expected, sitting slightly uneasily on top of the fresh clean taste. When you swallow, you'll feel a fizziness on your tongue if you stop to look for it.

Roodeberg

An odd cocktail of red grapes goes into this one. Cabernet Sauvignon, Syrah, Portugal's Tinto Barocca and the local Pinotage. On the bouquet there's a plummy note cut by grass and a hint of hay. To taste it's meaty and solid with an earthy – almost stony – quality. The fruit is a bit tough and lumbering, rounded off at the end with a hint of pepper.

Wine-growing area

Index

Abadia 105
Airen 106, 112
Aix-en-Provence, Coteaux d' 63
Alexander Valley 147
Aligoté
  Bulgaria 131
  France 43–4
Alsace 22, 32–5
Amarone della Valpolicella 88
Anjou 52–4
  white 19, 53
Anjou Gamay 22
Appellation Contrôlée 31–2, 36
Ardèche 22
  Vin de Pays des Coteaux de l' 59
Argentina 152–4
Armagnac 20
aroma see bouquet
Arruda 116
artichoke 152
Asenovgrad 136
asparagus 145, 152
Asti Spumante 20
Auckland 169
Australia 155–65
  wine classification 156
Austria 124–5
  wine classification 124, 131

Baden 102
Bairrada 116–17
Bandol 68
Barbaresco 23, 76–7
barbecued food 146
Barbera 77
Bardolino 77–8
Barolo 23, 78
Barossa Valley 163
Barsac 18
bass 47
Beaujolais 22, 49–52
Beaujolais Nouveau 50–1
Beaujolais-Villages 51
Beerenauslese 93
Bereich Berkastel 97
Bereich Kurfurstlay 97
Bergas 136
Bergerac 21, 69–70
Bianco di Custoza 79
blends 16–17, 18, 20
  Australia 165
Bordeaux 18, 21, 35–41
Bouches du Rhône, Vin de Pays des 59
bouquet 15; see also smelling
Bourgogne 44–5
Bourgogne Aligoté 43–4
Bourgogne Grand Ordinaire 42
Bourgogne Passe-Tout-Grains 44
Bourgueil 57
Brouilly 52
Brown Brothers 164
Brunello di Montalcino 79
Bulgaria 130–36
  wine classification 131
Bull's Blood 129, 137–8
Burgundy 22, 42–9

Cabernet d'Anjou 21, 54
Cabernet Franc 21
  Australia 157
  France 38, 41, 53, 69, 74
Cabernet Sauvignon 15, 20–1
  Argentina 153
  Australia 157
  Bulgaria 130, 131–2, 136

California 142–3
Chile 149–50
France 37, 38, 59, 63, 66, 68, 69, 74
Italy 80
Lebanon 128
New Zealand 167, 169
South Africa 171, 172
Spain 104, 105, 107
Yugoslavia 138
Cadillac 41
Cahors 70–1
California 22, 140–6
Cariñena 104
Carignan 23, 24, 59, 63, 64, 65, 66, 67, 69
Casa Portuguesa 120
casseroles 60, 69, 78, 108, 146
Castillo de Alhambra 106
Catarina 119
cauliflower cheese 61, 82
Cencibel see Tempranillo
Cesar 44
Chablis 45–6
Champagne 16, 17, 22, 26
charcuterie 71
Chardonnay 17, 18
  Australia 158, 161
  Austria 124
  Bulgaria 130, 131, 132–3
  California 143
  Chile 150–1
  France 42, 44, 45, 48, 49, 53, 59
  Italy 80
  New Zealand 162–3, 169
  Portugal 114–15
  Spain 104, 105, 107, 108
Château Grillet 58
Château la Jaubertie 70
Château Musar 21, 23, 128
Château Petrus 109
Châteauneuf-du-Pape 23, 59–60
cheese 58, 112, 158
  dishes 58
  herby 56
Chénas 51
Chenin Blanc 19
  Argentina 153
  Australia 164
  France 53
  New Zealand 162
  South Africa 171, 172
Chianti 20, 80
chicken 47, 56, 72, 121, 154
  salad 83
Chile 148–52
  wine classification 149
Chinese food 33
Chinon 57
Chiroubles 52
Cinsaut 23
  France 59, 63, 64, 65, 66
  Lebanon 128
  New Zealand 167
  South Africa 172
Clare Valley 163
classification
  Australia 56
  Austria 124
  Bulgaria 131
  Chile 149
  France 30, 31–2, 36–7, 42–3
  Germany 92–3
  Italy 75–6
  Portugal 115
  Spain 104

climate 26
Cognac 20
cold meats 53, 68, 150
Colombard 72, 73
colour 13
Condrieu 58
Controliran 131
Coonawarra 163
coq au vin 61
Corbières 64
corn on the cob 58
Cornas 22
Coronas 108
Corrida 103
Cortese 79, 82
Corvina 77, 88
Corvo 81
Costers del Segre 104–5
Costières de Nîmes 65–6
Côte Chalonnaise 46–7
Côte de Beaune Villages 46
Côte d'Or 47
Côte Rôtie 22
Coteaux d'Aix-en-Provence 63
Coteaux du Languedoc 66–7
Coteaux du Layon 19
Coteaux du Tricastin 63
Côtes de Provence 67–9
Côtes de St-Mont 74
Côtes du Frontonnais 71
Côtes du Lubéron 61
Côtes du Rhône 22, 23, 58, 61–2
Côtes du Roussillon 23, 69
Côtes du Ventoux 63
Country Wines 131
Courbu 73
crème de cassis 55, 131
crème de mûre 55, 131
crêpes
  savoury 79
Crianza 109
Criolla 153
Crozes-Hermitage
  Australia 159
  France 60
Cru 36, 43

Dão 115, 117–18
Deidesheim 100
Demestica 122–3
description 14–15
Deutscher Tafelwein 92
diethylene glycol 124
Dolcetto 81–2
Don Cortez 103
Douro 23, 118
Dry Creek 147
Dry Moscato 118–19
duck 48
Duras 72

Edelzwicker 32
Edna Valley 147
Eiswein 93
England 126–7
English wine 127
Entre-Deux-Mers 18, 36, 38–9
Europe, Eastern 129–39
Europe, Western 30–127

fermentation 24
fish 35, 56, 58, 63, 72, 73, 85, 89, 154
  oily 39, 44, 56
  pie 79
Fitou 65

Fleurie 51–2
France 30–74
  wine classification 30, 31–2, 36–7, 42–3
Franken 102
Frascati 20, 82
Friuli 83
Fronton see Côtes du Frontonnais
fruit 74
  tart 74
Fumé Blanc
  Australia 160, 164
  California 144–5
Gaillac 72
Galestro 20
Gamay 22, 42, 44, 45, 49, 53, 59
Gamay de Touraine 23
game 60, 78, 150, 162
Gamza 134, 136
Gard, Vin de Pays du 65–6
Gargenega 79, 86
Garnacha see Grenache
Garrafeira 115
Garrafeira 120
Gascogne, Vin de Pays des Côtes de 20,
  72–3
Gattinara 23
Gavi 82–3
Germany 91–102
  wine classification 92–3
Gewürztraminer
  Chile 149, 151
  France 32–3
  Germany 102
  New Zealand 167, 169
  Spain 108
Gigondas 61
Gisbourne 169
Givry 46
glasses 12
goulash 61, 138
Goulburn 164
Gran Reserva 109
Gran Viña Sol 108
grape concentrate 127
grape spirit 155
grape varieties 15–24
Graves 21, 36, 39
Grecheto 85
Greece 122–3
Grenache 23
  France 58, 62, 63, 64, 65, 66
  Spain 105, 107
Groslot 53
Grüner Veltliner 124–5
Gutedel 102
Gutenborner 127

ham 48, 133
hare 78
Hautes-Côtes de Beaune 47–8
Hautes-Côtes de Nuits 48
Hawke's Bay 169
l'Hérault, Vin de Pays de 66
Hermitage 60 and see Syrah
Hochheim 101
Hock Deutscher Tafelwein 97
Hungary 136–8
Hunter Valley 155, 161, 162

Italian salami 83
Italy 75–90
  wine classification 75–6

Jardin de la France, Vin de Pays du 54
João Pires 118
Johannisberg Riesling 101
José Maria da Fonseca 119
Juliénas 51
Jurançon 73–4

Kabinett 93
Kerner 94, 98
Khan Krum 132, 136
Kir 43–4
Korten 136
Kreuznach 102

La Mancha 105–6
lamb, roast 105

Lambrusco 83
Landwein 92
Languedoc, Coteaux du 66–7
Languedoc-Roussillon 20
lasagne 63
Lavon, Coteaux du 19
Laski Rizling 129, 138–9
latitudes 26–7
Lebanon 21, 23, 128
legends 24
Liebfraumilch 98, 100, 101, 102
Lirac 23
Loire 52–8
Loupiac 41
Lozitza 136
Lubéron, Côtes du 61
Lugana 84
Lugny 48

Macabeo 69
macaroni 82
macération carbonique 22, 61, 64, 72
mackerel 44
Mâcon 22
Mâcon-Blanc Villages 48
Mâcon Rouge 48
Malbec 69, 70
Malvasia 79, 82
Manseng, Grand and Petit 73
Margaret River 164
Margaux 40
Marlborough 170
Marqués de Cáceres 110
Marsanne
  Australia 159
  France 60
Mateus Rosé 120
Mauzac 72
Mavrud 133
McLaren Vale 164
meat
  pies 117
  red 63, 85, 111, 112, 120, 128
  tarts 117
  white 85, 160
Médoc 21, 36, 40
Mehana 133
Meia Pipa 119
Melnik 134, 136
Melon de Bourgogne see Muscadet
Menetou-Salon 56
Mercurey 47
Merlot 21
  Australia 157
  Bulgaria 130, 132, 134
  California 144
  France 38, 41, 59, 66, 69, 70, 74
  Hungary 137
  Italy 84
  Spain 104, 105
Midi 23
Minervois 67
Misket 130, 134
Mission grapes 140
Molinara 77
Monbazillac 18
Montagny 47
Montepulciano d'Abruzzo 84–5
Monterey 147
Morgon 52
Morio-Muskat 94
Moscato Spumante 20
Mosel Deutscher Tafelwein 98
Mosel-Saar-Ruwer 101
Moulin Touchais 19
Moulin-à-Vent 51
Mount Barker 164
Mourvèdre 63, 66
mousses, savoury 58
Mudge 163
Müller-Thurgau 19
  England 127
  Germany 93, 95, 97, 98, 100, 101, 102
  New Zealand 166, 169
Muscadet 54–5
Muscat 19–20
  Australia 159

Bulgaria 130
France 33
Hungary 137
New Zealand 169
Portugal 119
Spain 108
Muscat de Beaumes de Venise 20, 58, 155
Muscat de Frontignan 20
Muskat 135

Nahe 102
Napa Valley 147
Navarra 23, 106–7
Nebbiolo 23, 76, 78
Negrette 71
New South Wales 162
New Zealand 166–70
Niersteiner 100
Niersteiner Gutes Domtal 99
North America 140–7
Novi Pazar 136
nut cutlet 62
nut roast 138

offal 71, 128
Oregon 22
Oriachovitza 136
Oriental food 33, 94, 151
Orvieto 20, 85
oysters 49

Padthaway 163
Parellada 108
Passe Tous-Grains 22
pasta 64, 80
pâtés 58, 68
Penedès 23, 107–8
Perquita 119–20
Pesquera 109
Pessac-Léognan 39
phylloxera 16, 109, 149
Piesporter Michelsberg 93, 97, 99
pilaf 53
pine resin 123
Pinot Blanc 33
  see also Weisser Burgunder
  Austria 124
  Germany 96
Pinot Grigio 85–6
Pinot Gris
  France 33–4
  Germany 102
Pinot Nero see Pinot Noir
Pinot Noir 22
  Bulgaria 136
  California 144
  England 127
  France 34, 42, 44, 45, 48, 59
  Germany 102
  New Zealand 167
  South Africa 172
Pinotage 167, 172
pizza 64
Plovdiv 136
Pomerol 21
pork 48, 158
Portugal 114–21
  wine classification 115
Pouilly-Fuissé 49
Pouilly-Fumé 18, 55–6
Premières Côtes de Bordeaux 40–1
Provence 20, 23
  Côtes de 67–9
puddings 74

Qualitätswein 92–3
quality see classification
quiches 150
Quinta da Bacalhoa 119

Raimat 104
red meat 63, 85, 111, 112, 120, 128
Regaliali 81
Regnié 52
Reichensteiner 127
Reserva 109
Reserve 131
Retsina 123
Rheingau 101

Rheinhessen 100
Rheinpfalz 100–101
Rhône 22, 58–63
Côtes du 22, 23, 58, 61–2
Ribera Del Duero 108–9
Riesling 17–18, 19
Argentina 153
Australia 159–60
Bulgaria 130, 135
Chile 149, 151–2
France 34–5
Germany 93, 95, 97, 98, 100, 101, 102
Italy 79
New Zealand 167
Rioja 23, 109–10
risotto 79, 87
Riverina 162
Riverland 163–4
roast meats 67, 77, 105, 108, 146, 150, 154
Rondinella 77
Roodeberg 172
Roussillon, Côtes du 23, 69
Rueda 110–11
Ruländer see Pinot Gris
Rully 46
Ruppertsberg 100
Russian River 147

Saint-Amour 51
St Chinian 67
St-Emilion 21, 36, 41
St-Estèphe 41
St-Joseph 22, 159
St-Laurent 124
St-Mont, Côtes de 74
St-Nicholas-de-Bourgeuil 57
St-Peray 159
St-Véran 49
Ste-Croix-du-Mont 41
Sakar 131, 136
salad 53, 150
chicken 83
salmon 56, 63, 158
smoked 83
San Luis Obispo 147
Sancerre 18, 56
Sangiovese 80
Santa Barbara 147
Santa Maria 147
Santa Ynez 147
Saumur 19
sausages 68, 78, 83
Sauvignon Blanc 15
Australia 160
Bulgaria 135
California 144–5
Chile 149, 152
France 56
New Zealand 168, 170
Spain 111
Sauvignon de Touraine 18
Sauvignon-de-St-Bris 18
Scheurebe 95
Schloss Böckelheim 102
Schonburger 127

seafood 39, 63, 73, 83, 89, 97
selection de grains nobles 34
Sémillon 18
Australia 18, 160–1
France 69, 70
shellfish 49
shepherd's pie 61, 62
Shiraz see Syrah
Shumen 136
Sin Crianza 109
Sliven 136
smell see bouquet
smelling 11–12, 13
smoked food 133
smoked salmon 83
Soave 20, 86
Sogrape 120
soil 26
sole 154
Sonoma County 147
soup 68, 133
South Africa 171–2
South America 148–54
spaghetti 78, 113
bolognese 62, 63, 153
Spain 103–13
wine classification 104
Spanna see Nebbiolo
Spätburgunder see Pinot Noir
Spätlese 93
Stambolovo 134, 136
steak 77
steak and kidney 61
Steen see Chenin Blanc
stews 67, 71, 77, 133, 138
stir-fries 119
Suhindol 131, 136
sulphur 53, 55, 99
superiore 78
Svischtov 131, 136
Swan Valley 164
Sylvaner 19
France 35
Germany 96, 98, 100, 102
Syrah 22–3
Australia 157–8, 161
France 59, 60, 62, 63, 64, 65
Lebanon 128

Tannat 70, 74
tannin 15, 16, 20, 25, 64, 76, 142
taste 12, 13–14, 15
tasting 11–15
Tavel 23, 62
Tempranillo 23, 105, 106, 107, 108, 109, 112
Teroldego Rotaliano 86
Terra Alta
Tinto de Anfora 119
Tinto de Toro 111
Tinto Velho 120
Tocai 79, 87
Tokay d'Alsace see Pinot Gris
Tokay, Hungary 137
Toro 111
Torrontes 153, 154
Torres 107, 108

Touraine 57
Touraine Gamay 57
Touraine Sauvignon 57
Trebbiano 20
Bulgaria 130
Italy 72, 79, 82, 84, 85, 86, 87
Tres Torres Sangredetoro 108
Tressot 44
Tricastin, Coteaux du 63
Trocken 99
Trockenbeerenauslese 93
trout 44
turbot 47
turkey 128

Ugni Blanc see Trebbiano
United States of America 140–7

Vacqueyras 61
Valdepeñas 23, 111–12
Valencia 112–13
Valpolicella 87–8
Vega Sicilia 108
vegetable casseroles and pies 34, 58, 64
vegetarian dishes 69
vendange tardive 34
Veneto 21
venison 78, 162
Ventoux, Côtes du 63
Verdejo 110
Verdicchio 20, 88–9
Vermentino 65, 89
Vernaccia di San Gimignano 89–90
Victoria 164
Vin d'Alsace 32
Vin de Corse 64–5
Vin de Pays 31
Vin de Pays de l'Hérault 66
Vin de Pays des Bouches du Rhône 59
Vin de Pays des Coteaux de l'Ardèche 59
Vin de Pays des Côtes de Gascogne 20, 72–3
Vin de Pays du Gard 65–6
Vin de Pays du Jardin de la France 54
Vin de Table 31
Vin Délimité de Qualité Supérieur 31
Viña Esmeralda 108
Viña Sol 108
Vinho Verde 115, 120–1
Vino Nobile di Montepulciano 90
Viognier 58
Viré 48
vitis labrusca 140
vitis vinifera 15–16, 166
Vouvray 19, 57–8

Washington State 22
weather see climate
Weisser Burgunder 96
see also Pinot Blanc
white meat 85, 160
wine-growing sites 26–7

yeast 24
Yugoslavia 138–9

Zenato 86
Zinfandel 145–6

For a list of specific recommendations of wine to try, write to the following address enclosing an sae:

Taste of Wine
Room A3134
BBC Enterprises Ltd
Woodlands
80 Wood Lane
LONDON W12 0TT